Mindi Wroblewski is a woman with a heart for the things of God. Her book on Genesis is a deep draught of Biblical truth and self-examination. It's part devotional part commentary, in which she asks straightforward reasonable questions, identifying the foundational truths upon which any truly Biblical worldview must be based. She doesn't shy away from difficult interpretive questions, letting the Word of God be its own interpreter. If you are willing to join Mindi in her deep dive into Genesis, you find lessons, insights, and boatloads of truth. And you will come away knowing God better than you did before.

—Frank Wright, Ph.D.,
President & CEO D. James Kennedy Ministries

The author of *Daily Reflections, Finding our Identity in Genesis*, makes the book of Genesis come alive! She walks you back through history, raising relevant questions along the way. The way it's written, she makes the stories of old seem just as relevant today. If you don't think you have that much in common with the characters in Genesis, think again. Mindi beautifully connects their stories to the very things we can struggle with today.

—Tammy Hernandez,
Author of *Soul Beliefs, Removing the Obstacles That Prevent Intimacy and Breakthrough*

Daily Reflections is not a book I would grab in the morning for a quick inspirational blurb to lift my spirits or to get my thoughts going in the right direction, although those can be beneficial. Rather, because I need a face-to-face encounter with God through a deeper examination of what He has laid out for us in His Word, I frequently choose this book written by someone who has spent many hours mining the Scriptures for gold.

Mindi has a God-given talent for directing others toward a better grasp of what God has spoken, toward a "knowledge of God's will in all spiritual wisdom and understanding," as the Apostle Paul prayed for the early Christians. If you're ready to spend a little more time meditating on the richness of Scripture, this is a book you will find most helpful.

—Donna Pharr Sparks,
Teacher (Ret'd) and freelance writer for Family Circle and Women's Day Magazines, as well as curriculum study guides

DAILY REFLECTIONS

To Emily,
Enjoy the journey
Through Genesis!
God bless
Mandi

DAILY REFLECTIONS

Finding Our Identity in Genesis

MINDI WROBLEWSKI

Copyright © 2020 by Mindi Wroblewski

All rights reserved.

No part of this book may be reproduced in any form or by any electronic or mechanical means, including information storage and retrieval systems, without written permission from the author, except for the use of brief quotations in a book review.

Scriptures marked NKJV are taken from the NEW KING JAMES VERSION®. Copyright© 1982 by Thomas Nelson, Inc. Used by permission. All rights reserved.

ISBN: 978-1-953314-06-2

Library of Congress Control Number: 2020916045

Printed by: BookMobile in the USA.

Published by:

Messenger Books
1629 Brookhollow, Dr.
Lindale, TX 75771

Messengerbooks.com

To my best friend and husband, Tom, whose love and support have made this journey possible.

CONTENTS

Introduction	xiii
1. Day 1	1
2. Day 2	5
3. Day 3	7
4. Day 4	10
5. Day 5	12
6. Day 6	14
7. Day 7	16
8. Day 8	18
9. Day 9	20
10. Day 10	22
11. Day 11	25
12. Day 12	28
13. Day 13	30
14. Day 14	32
15. Day 15	34
16. Day 16	36
17. Day 17	38
18. Day 18	41
19. Day 19	43
20. Day 20	45
21. Day 21	47
22. Day 22	49
23. Day 23	51
24. Day 24	53
25. Day 25	55
26. Day 26	57
27. Day 27	59
28. Day 28	61
29. Day 29	63
30. Day 30	65
31. Day 31	67

32. Day 32	70
33. Day 33	72
34. Day 34	74
35. Day 35	77
36. Day 36	79
37. Day 37	81
38. Day 38	83
39. Day 39	85
40. Day 40	87
41. Day 41	90
42. Day 42	92
43. Day 43	94
44. Day 44	96
45. Day 45	98
46. Day 46	100
47. Day 47	103
48. Day 48	105
49. Day 49	108
50. Day 50	110
51. Day 51	113
52. Day 52	115
53. Day 53	118
54. Day 54	120
55. Day 55	122
56. Day 56	124
57. Day 57	127
58. Day 58	130
59. Day 59	133
60. Day 60	136
61. Day 61	138
62. Day 62	141
63. Day 63	144
64. Day 64	146
65. Day 65	150
66. Day 66	153
67. Day 67	156
68. Day 68	159
69. Day 69	162
70. Day 70	165

71. Day 71	168
72. Day 72	171
73. Day 73	174
74. Day 74	177
75. Day 75	179
76. Day 76	182
77. Day 77	185
78. Day 78	188
79. Day 79	191
80. Day 80	194
81. Day 81	197
82. Day 82	200
83. Day 83	203
84. Day 84	206
85. Day 85	209
86. Day 86	211
87. Day 87	213
88. Day 88	217
89. Day 89	220
90. Day 90	223
91. Day 91	226
92. Day 92	229
93. Day 93	232
94. Day 94	235
95. Day 95	238
96. Day 96	241
97. Day 97	244
98. Day 98	246
99. Day 99	248
100. Day 100	251
Afterword	255
Notes	259
About the Author	263

INTRODUCTION

When people write books, it's not just words on a page that have no meaning or purpose. There are chapters in each book that tell a story—fiction, non-fiction, instruction, or teaching on whatever issue is being written about. There's a beginning, a middle, and an end. The Bible is not any different, except it is a compilation of inspired books telling God's story to us, His creation. When we read it from that perspective, it can do amazing things for us. We can discover who we are, why we are here, and what we are meant to do with our lives because we learn who is behind this crazy thing we call life. The wonderful truth is, God is not crazy, but life is crazy without Him. I've read through the Bible many times, and each time I learn something new.

Several years ago, as I was reading through the Bible, I felt a call to write a devotional on the Old Testament. Why? It's the foundation upon which the New Testament is built. If we don't know and understand the Old Testament, how on earth are we going to understand the New? It would be like building a house without first laying a foundation. The house will eventually tumble down. Understanding the Old Testament is essential for every believer.

Originally I envisioned a yearly devotional through the entire Old Testament. In 2016, I began a FaceBook group named, "Daily Reflections," and began posting my writings. For two-plus years, I studied and wrote my reflections, beginning in Genesis to the last chapter of Malachi, and completed what I thought was a writer's Picasso! It sat on my computer for another two years; my heart wanted to publish it, but my mind found excuse after excuse not to. As I began editing, I realized that I had neglected Genesis, the book most foundational to our New Testament faith! I became discouraged. My heart didn't have the strength to put more time and effort into it. I began to try, but by the time I got to Chapter 22, I had fifty days of devotions. How in the world was the entire Old Testament going to fit into a one-year devotional without the book being one foot thick? I remember going to my husband, Tom, who is not a writer, but couldn't be more supportive of my desire to write. I said to him, "I want to do this devotional, but I'm discouraged and feel so alone; like I need a group of mentors or someone who can push me to do this."

A week or two later, I received an email inviting me to join *Unlocking Your Book*. At first, I hesitated, but then felt the Lord urging me to join. "Go for it, if you think it will help," were the encouraging words I needed to hear from Tom. It was the best thing I could have done. Jeremiah Yancy and Krissy Nelson are enthusiastic, uplifting, full of ideas, and, most importantly, love Jesus with all of their hearts. They encouraged all of their would-be writers to seek God's heart in their endeavor to write a book.

As time went by quickly, and days passed, I didn't get anything done. I got discouraged once again. I shared all of this with my wonderful husband, and he suggested, "Why don't you just do a devotional on Genesis." At first, I didn't like the idea, but the more I thought and prayed about it, the more the answer was a clear, "Yes." I tell this story because when God puts something on our hearts, whatever it may be, He doesn't always give us the big picture or the smallest details that go along with it. When I began, I studied and wrote on the Old Testament with the intent of doing a one-year devotional, but it has become much more than that.

Genesis is the foundational book of our Christian faith. In it, we find our origins. If we don't know the book of Genesis, we don't know where we came from. More importantly, if we don't understand what happened when Adam and Eve disobeyed God by eating from the Tree of Knowledge of Good and Evil, we don't understand sin. If we don't understand sin, we don't know why we need a Savior. If we don't know why we need a Savior, then it's up to us to figure life out for ourselves, which ultimately leads to death and everlasting darkness; separation from our Creator for eternity.

The Old Testament also reveals the history of God's people, *His* Story, and the blood covenant He made with Abraham in Genesis. Without the shedding of blood, there can be no remission for our sins. When going beyond Genesis through the entire Old Testament, we come to understand that sacrificing the blood of animals for our sins was never enough - it takes so much more! This is why Jesus Christ, the Son of God, was sent to earth: to die for our sins once and for all. The discovery of God's secrets in Genesis opens our eyes to the truth of who we are, why we are here, and where we are going.

I am hopeful that by beginning with the very first book of the Old Testament, it will be helpful to know the history of how God chose a people and His purpose in doing so. Genesis is a book filled with people's lives and how God directed them. Some were obedient, some were disobedient. They all have character flaws, just like each one of us has character flaws. They are all people who God used in a special way for His purposes, and He does the same thing with us today. Though none of us are in the Bible, He still calls us by name and has a plan for our lives (John 10:3; Isaiah 43:1).

I have learned so much about our Heavenly Father through this entire process, and I am excited to pass this understanding and knowledge on to others. I'm no scholar, teacher, or philosopher, but I do have a heart for Jesus and a longing and desire to know Him more. I know that the way to do that is by reading what is written in His profound book that teaches us not only who we are, but also who God wants us to be and who we can become in Him.

My prayer is that you will discover more about your identity in God and His great love for you as we study Genesis together.

Because of the Love of Christ,

Mindi

DAY 1

OUR IDENTITY

"In Him we live and move and have our being, as also some of your own poets have said, 'For we are also His offspring.'"
(Acts 17:28, NKJV)

Is your identity found in the work you do, where you live, or perhaps in your relationship with others? Have you ever asked the question, "Who am I?" As a child, and even into young adulthood, I had difficulty with my identity. My dad was a professional football player for the San Francisco 49ers and I was often referred to as "Dan's daughter." In my teen years I began wondering if I'd always live in the shadow of my dad's notoriety.

My first "real job" as a cashier in a drug store gave me an inkling of whether or not I would live under my father's identity. After working there for several months, I removed my last name from my name tag. I discovered that I didn't get the usual attention that came when I was associated with my locally famous father. At first I liked it, but it wasn't long until I started asking myself, "So, who am I? Where did I come from, and why am I here?" I began looking for ways to answer those questions, but nothing satisfied me on the inside. It wasn't until soon after my 20th birthday I was introduced to someone who changed my life forever.

Fast forward to the present, I am now in my sixth decade and more in love than ever with that special someone I met so long ago. Who is He and what is His name? He is the Son of the Living God and His name is Jesus. He is the most unique Man in human history. He came to earth for one reason, to die for my sins and the sins of the world. "He was pierced for our transgressions; He was crushed for our iniquities… and the Lord has laid on Him the iniquity of us all" (Isaiah 53:5-6). Not only is He God, but He was a man, born of a virgin. Hundreds of years earlier, Isaiah foretold the Messiah's birth in the Old Testament. "Therefore the Lord Himself will give you a sign: The virgin will be with child and will give birth to a son and will call Him Immanuel" (Isaiah 7:14), which means "God with us."

When Jesus was thirty years old, He went into the desert where He was tempted by the devil (Luke 4:1-2). After forty days of prayer and fasting, He went to Nazareth, the town where He was raised. On the Sabbath day, He went into the synagogue, as this was His custom. The scroll of the prophet Isaiah was handed to him. Unrolling it, he found the place where it was written:

The Spirit of the Lord is on Me, because He has anointed me to preach good news to the poor. He has sent Me to proclaim freedom for the prisoners and recovery of sight for the blind, to release the oppressed, to proclaim the year of the Lord's favor (Isaiah 61:1-2).

He rolled up the scroll, sat down, and said, "Today this scripture is fulfilled in your hearing" (Luke 4:16-21). The time came for Jesus to begin His earthly ministry.

When Jesus was brought before Pilate and accused of insurrection, the Jewish people shouted "Crucify Him." Pilate asked, "Shall I crucify your king?" The chief priests answered, "We have no king but Caesar." Finally, Pilate handed him over to be crucified (John 19:15-16). He was nailed to a cross as was foretold in Psalm 22:16, "A band of evil men has encircled Me. They have pierced my hands and my feet." Also as foretold, they divided His garments among them and cast lots for His clothing (Psalm 22:18).

After three days in the grave, He rose from the dead. He appeared to Peter and then to the 12 (apostles). After that, He appeared to more than 500 (1 Corinthians 15:3-8). He ascended into heaven and is at God's right hand, with angels, authorities and powers in submission to Him (1 Peter 3:22).

He is coming back again. When He returns, His feet will stand on the Mount of Olives, east of Jerusalem, and the Mount of Olives will be split in two from east to west, forming a great valley...Then the Lord my God will come, and all the holy ones with Him. On that day living water will flow out from Jerusalem...The Lord will be king over the whole earth. On that day there will be one Lord, and His name the only Name (Zechariah 14:4-5, and 8-9).

The Old Testament prophecies about Jesus were written centuries before they occurred. According to the Good News Dispatch, the chances of even eight of them coming to pass is:

$$1 \text{ in } 10 \text{ to the } 28^{th} \text{ power}$$

or 1 in 10,000,000,000,000,000,000,000,000,000. I don't know about you, but I don't even have a name for that number! Those are pretty low odds, yet four of the six prophecies I've referred to are documented in the New Testament as having already taken place. If that isn't evidence enough for Jesus Christ being who He said He is, then I'm speechless. Another resource is *The Case for Christ,* by Lee Strobel, a former atheist who set out on a quest to prove Jesus was a phony but came away with a much different conclusion.

You might ask, *How is all of this important to my identity?* Listen, if Jesus is who He says He is, and He died in my place for my sins; if He forgave my sins and cleansed me from my unrighteousness, then He is the One in whom I find my identity because I am now dead to my sinful ways and my life is now hidden with Christ in God. And when Christ, who is my life, appears, then I will also appear with Him in glory (Colossians 3:3). I am a child of God (Galatians 3:26-29).

My motivation behind writing this devotional is that if we can know the God of the Old Testament, we can know the Jesus of the New Testament, the One who gives us our true identity (Acts 17:28).

DAY 2

IN THE BEGINNING
Read Genesis 1:1-2

Have you ever asked the question: Where did I come from? If science is right, we either morphed into humans from apes over millions of years, or the Big Bang occurred and we were part of that. How did it happen? Was there anyone who witnessed any of this, who wrote it all down and can say with 100 percent certainty this is the way it came about? If we came from nothing, does that mean when we die we go to nothing? And why do we have to die?

Does anyone know of anything that just appeared on the scene of its own accord in our lifetimes? Or does someone first come up with an idea, create a plan for it, performing experiments and tests until it works, and then ultimately they implement the result of that idea? Things like electricity, airplanes, cars, buildings, washing machines and dryers, just to name a few? Was there not some means by which all of these things came into existence? Are there not writings that give descriptions so others can read about their origins?

Why do human beings with the unique ability to reason exist? And why do we have the ability to think up an endless array of products to make life easier and better? Why are we the only species that can communicate by speech and/or writing? Why are there two genders and not three, four or five? Why do we have feelings and emotions? Where does our understanding of what is right and wrong come from? Where does love come from, and why do we long to love and be loved?

Is there a source for the answers to these questions? I believe there is. It is not a scientific book, determining the method of how and when things happened, but it is a revelation of how we got here, how we should live, and where we are going. Open the book and the first three words are: "In the beginning." Then the words that follow this unique opening reveal the beginning to which it refers: "...God created the heavens and the earth. Now the earth was formless and empty; darkness was over the surface of the deep and the Spirit of God was hovering over the waters."

In the beginning, was the Word, and the Word was with God, and the Word was God. He was with God in the beginning. Through Him all things were made; without Him, nothing was made that has been made (John 1:1-3).

To this very day we refer to our planet as the earth, and most everyone on it believes in something called heaven. It is the Creator who gives eye witness to the account of how it all began, for He was there as the events unfolded.

Heavenly Father, we are just starting this journey into how the world began. I ask for Your wisdom and understanding. Open my heart to the revelation of Your word, which gives answers to where we came from, who we are, why we are here, and where we are going. I ask all of this in the name of Jesus. Amen.

DAY 3

HE FIRST AND SECOND DAYS – SEPARATION
Read Genesis 1:3-8

God began speaking and things happened. First, there was light. No sun, moon and stars are mentioned. So where did the light come from? John 1:4 tells us, "In Him was life, and that life was the light of men. The light shines in the darkness, but the darkness has not understood it."

Darkness was dispelled by the light and presence of Jesus Christ (the Word) on that very first day. If we take it one step further, Revelation 21:23 tells us, "The city (New Jerusalem) does not need the sun or the moon to shine on it, for the glory of God gives it light, and the Lamb is its lamp." He (Jesus) was there in the beginning; He is there at the end; and His light will shine throughout all eternity.

As the Spirit of God hovered over the waters, God said, "Let there be an expanse between the waters to separate water from water. So God made the expanse and separated the water under the expanse from the water above it, and it was so. God called the expanse 'sky.' And there was evening, and there was morning, the second day."

If you go outside and look up, planting your feet firmly on the ground, tilting your head slightly back and eyes looking up, you will see an unending expanse above us called "the sky." Above the sky, beyond our ability to see with the naked eye, or even with the help of a telescope, is heaven. Below the sky, where we stand, is earth. We are told both places have water. We know that without water, we cannot exist more than a few days. The water on earth sustains our life; however, there is another type of water, a spiritual water, which Jesus told us about during his encounter with a Samaritan woman.

Sitting on a plot of land known as Jacob's well, Jesus saw a woman coming to draw water. He asked her, "Will you give me a drink?" She was taken aback by his request as Jews did not talk to Samaritans, especially women. But He answered her by saying, "If you knew the gift of God and who it is that asks you for a drink, you would have asked him and he would have given you living water." Astonished at His response, she said, "Sir, you have nothing to draw with and the well is deep. Where can you get this living water?" Jesus answered, "Everyone who drinks this water (from the well) will be thirsty again, but whoever drinks the water I give him will never thirst. Indeed, the water I give him will become in him a spring of water welling up to eternal life" (John 4:4-14). The water which God provides on earth sustains us, but the living water which Jesus promises gives us eternal life.

Lord, thank You that I can rest in the knowledge that You are my Creator and You know everything about me, my needs, my wants and my desires. You have the answers to my questions and You desire me to know

You in an intimate way. Draw me into Your presence as we journey through Your word from the very beginning of time. In the name of Jesus, I pray. Amen.

DAY 4

THE THIRD DAY – GOD'S INVISIBLE QUALITIES
Read Genesis 1:9-13

The Lord was very busy on the third day. Not only did the earth take its form but He gathered the water under the sky to one place and dry ground appeared. Ezekiel 43:2 proclaims, "…and I saw the glory of the God of Israel coming from the east. His voice was like the roar of rushing waters, and the land was radiant with His glory." When God spoke, and the land and sea separated, the sound must have been deafening, more than the roar of a thousand oceans at one time. The majesty of God's presence on the earth produced not only land, but mountains and valleys, canyons and caves, and waterfalls streaming down the mountainsides into the creeks and rivers down below. The beauty and grandeur of it all must have been breathtaking. When God finished, He saw that it was good and, as a once-popular song proclaimed, "It's only just begun."

Then God said, "Let the land produce vegetation: seed-bearing plants and trees on the land that bear fruit with seed in it, according to their various kinds." And it was so. There are so many varieties and kinds of plants, flowers, trees and vegetables on the earth, it would take more than a person's lifetime to know them all. Not only did God create all of these plants, flowers and trees, but each one has within it seed for reproducing. So it wasn't a one-time event, but it was meant to be perpetual. God was preparing the earth to be inhabited. He knew what was needed, and He saw that it was good.

If we want to know who our heavenly Father is, all we have to do is look around and see his creation. The earth remains with its land and seas. God's invisible qualities - His eternal power and divine nature – have been clearly seen, being understood from what has been made, so that men are without excuse (Romans 1:20).

It's sad to think that many will die without ever meeting the Creator of the universe until they go into eternity, when there is a book that tells us what we need to know without spending a lifetime trying to figure it out. God is real. He is mighty. He is all-knowing and all-powerful. There is no one like Him. Apart from Him, there is no God (Isaiah 44:24 & 45:6).

Lord, thank you for the simplicity with which You have revealed Your creation. Thank You that we don't need a dissertation or multi-page explanation as to how it all began. Help me receive what You have so freely given. In the name of Jesus, I pray. Amen.

DAY 5

THE FOURTH DAY – THE SUN, MOON AND STARS
Read Genesis 1:14-19

There are hundreds, if not thousands, of books written about the moon, the sun, the stars, the planets and their effect on life. For those who don't want to acknowledge the existence of God, there's certainly a plethora of research and conclusions to turn to. For those who believe in God, there are also many resources to turn to, including an interesting article written by the Institute for Creation Research, "Planet Earth: Plan or Accident," which describes the perfection of the earth's placement exactly where it is.[1]

There are those who call themselves psychics or fortune-tellers who make millions of dollars looking into crystal balls or reading palms, saying they can see the stars and planets, and predict the future based on their placement when a person was born. They may think they have the ability to do these things but they did not create the sun, the moon, and the stars. It was God who spoke them into existence, saying they would serve as signs to mark seasons, days and years, governing the day and night by the intensity of their light.

In the book of Job, he says, "God spreads out the northern skies over empty space; and He suspends the earth over nothing." He goes on, "God wraps up the waters in His clouds: yet the clouds do not burst under their weight. He covers the face of the full moon, spreading His clouds over it. He marks out the horizon on the face of the waters for a boundary between light and dark...and these are but the fringe of His work" (Job 26:7-14).

When we look into the sky, there is the sun during the day; the moon, stars and planets at night. There is a universe, a solar system, perhaps many solar systems, but we have yet to discover life anywhere but on earth, and that is because God planned it that way.

There are heavenly bodies and there are earthly bodies, but the splendor of the heavenly bodies is one kind and the splendor of the earthly bodies is another. The sun has one kind of splendor, the moon another and the stars another; and star differs from star in splendor (1 Corinthians 15:40-41). "...the Lord made the heavens. Splendor and majesty are before Him; strength and glory are in His sanctuary" (Psalm 96:4-6).

Lord, may the eyes of my heart be enlightened in order that I may know the hope to which You have called me, the riches of Your glorious inheritance in the saints and Your incomparably great power to those who believe (Ephesians 1:18). In the name of Jesus, I pray. Amen.

DAY 6

THE FIFTH DAY - OCEANS AND BIRDS
Read Genesis 1:20-23

What is hidden below the surface of the waters is so different from what exists on earth. It's not easy to understand how the creatures of the sea survive. It's a mystery that has been explored by many, including the famous Jacque Cousteau, who spent his entire life studying and exploring the sea and the creatures that live within it. During his lifetime, he used divers with cameras to capture whales, sharks, eels, and so much more to share with the world, but he couldn't capture it all. According to a website named "The Beach Chair Scientist," in the year 2000, a census was begun to determine what lives in the ocean. Over 2,000 scientists from 82 countries came together to answer this question, and according to this study, as of November 21, 2008, there are 230,000 known marine creatures that are described as "unique." Did Jacques Cousteau create them? Did scientists from all over the world create them? Where did they come from?

We need look no further than Genesis 1:20. In addition to the sea life, there are the different species and subspecies of birds. They come in all shapes, sizes and colors. Some can fly, some cannot. According to more than one website, there are 9,000 to 10,000 species of birds in the world, maybe even double that. It would take more than 2,000 scientists from all over the world to learn the intricate details of each species.

In Psalm 24:1, King David proclaimed, "The earth is the Lord's and everything in it, the world, and all who live in it; for He founded it upon the seas and established it upon the waters." If we believe this, we can enjoy all that He created on earth, into eternity, where He tells us, "Eye has not seen, nor ear heard, the things that the Lord has prepared for those who love Him" (1 Corinthians 2:9).

As Psalm 148:7 proclaims: Praise the Lord from the earth, you great sea creatures and all ocean depths, you wild animals and all cattle, small creatures and flying birds, praise the name of the Lord for His name alone is exalted; His splendor is above the earth and the heavens.

Lord, what was it like to create these glorious things on the earth? Were you singing as you created them? Were you shouting with joy? Were you laughing with excitement? May I be so bold as to ask that You bring me into Your mighty presence, reveal to me Your glory and the magnificence of who You are, my Creator, my Lord and my King. In the name of Jesus, I pray. Amen.

DAY 7

THE SIXTH DAY - CREATION CONTINUES
Read Genesis 1:24-31

On day six, God said, "Let the land produce living creatures according to their kinds: livestock, creatures that move along the ground, and wild animals, each according to its kind," and it was so. And God saw that it was good, but He wasn't finished. Someone was needed to care for all of God's handiwork. Then God said, "Let us make man in our image, in our likeness." So God created man in His own image; male and female He created them. God blessed them and said, "Be fruitful and increase in number; fill the earth and subdue it. Rule over the fish of the sea and the birds of the air and over every living creature that moves on the ground. I give you every seed-bearing plant on the face of the whole earth and every tree that has fruit with seed in it. They will be yours for food..." And it was so.

Wow, a lot happened on day six, which culminated with a clear instruction from God that He was putting man and woman in charge of all His creation. In our world today, that notion has been turned on its head. Animals, trees, plants, even food have come to the forefront of our everyday life, so much so that some people make them more important than their fellow human beings. On the contrary, it was for us that all of these things were created; not the other way around. Perhaps it's because we are so far removed from when God created us that we are making up our own rules to live by. It's like a child, who has no life experience, saying to their parents, "I don't have to do anything you say because you don't know anything!" That would not go over very well in many families.

It's my hope that by delving into what God has said, for He was there before the very beginning, we will gain a greater appreciation and understanding of how life is intended to be lived. Blessed is the man who trusts in the Lord, whose confidence is in Him (Jeremiah 17:7). We can trust Him because He is God (Psalm 3:5-8), and if we listen, He will teach us what we need to know about this wonderful thing called life.

Lord, help me trust in You with all of my heart and lean not to my own understanding. In all of my ways help me to acknowledge You, knowing You will make my paths straight (Proverbs 3:6). In the name of Jesus, I pray. Amen.

DAY 8

NO GOD BUT GOD
Re-read Genesis 1

*M*ore than likely, Moses was one of the most highly educated people of his time, having been raised in a palace by Pharaoh, who was the king of Egypt, and taught by the most brilliant minds who were available at Pharaoh's beck and call. So who better to write down the account of creation than Moses? But he wasn't there, you might say. How could he know all this? Not only were these events handed down from generation to generation, but God was there. These are the things that no one but God could know, and I believe He inspired Moses to write them down for all to read.

This may lead to another question like: How do we know it happened this way if no human was there? The prophet Isaiah tells us, "I am God, and there is no other; I am God, and there is none like me. I make known the end from the beginning, from ancient times, what is still to come... What I have said, that will I bring about; what I have planned, that will I do" (46:9). If there is no other God but God, who has always existed and cannot lie (Hebrews 6:18), then He was there and He alone can testify that what He made actually happened, and that it was good.

There are those who might ask, "How could God have always existed?" It can be a little confusing, even result in circular thinking that has no end, but there is a way to find out. In a court of law, there is something called "circumstantial evidence," which means you can conclude certain facts by the circumstances. The book of Genesis tells us that in the beginning, God was there. In the book of Revelation, the last book of the Bible, Jesus confirms this when He says, "I am the Alpha (the beginning) and the Omega (the end), who is and who was and who is to come, the Almighty" (Revelation 1:8). This is the circumstantial evidence that can lead us to conclude that God was, is, and always will be. From the beginning to the end, He was there.

We can debate this until our dying breath, but what good would it be to gain the whole world, yet forfeit our soul? For what can a person give in exchange for his very soul? (Matthew 16:24-25). The answer is: *nothing*. All the answers we need for life are contained in this one book.

Without faith it is IMPOSSIBLE to please God, because anyone who comes to Him must believe that He exists and that He rewards those who earnestly seek Him (Hebrews 11:6).

All we are asked to do is receive what God says, to believe not only what He says, but what He has done, and to live it. Jesus, our Lord and Savior, has done the rest (Ephesians 1:11-14).

Lord, may my heart take delight in knowing that You are the One true God and that what You say You will do. I can count on it! Amen.

DAY 9

A DAY OF REST
Read Genesis 2:1-2

Does anyone today know what it means to really rest? God did. In six days He created the earth with waters, lands, mountains, valleys, birds, sea creatures, cattle, creatures that move along the ground and wild animals, according to their various kinds. He laid the foundation which would enable the man and woman He created to live in His perfect world and to take care of it all.

Not that God needed a physical rest because He was exhausted, but because He finished what He began. It was time to stop His work and enjoy His creation. How often do we do that, if at all? I know I am guilty of constantly being on the go. Even as a Christian, there was a time when I rarely rested. My job as a court reporter was demanding both in federal court and on Capitol Hill. I worked long hours, and the weekends were my opportunity to relax. I didn't attend church very often on Sunday because I had other things to do. I justified my behavior, but deep down I knew I was not pleasing the Lord.

Even if we don't read or know the Bible, we know we need rest. Turn on the television, read the paper, go on the internet, you can get exhausted searching for places to find rest and relaxation. Even taking a short vacation for a few days can bring with it a tension that takes away the pleasure of "getting away." On the other hand, in God's case, He blessed the seventh day and made it a holy day for resting, and that has never changed.

When Sunday comes this week, take the day to consider what God meant to rest and keep the day holy. Let Him speak to your heart and He will make it clear how He wants you to accomplish this at the end of a busy six days' work. Anyone who enters God's rest also rests from his own work, just as God did from His (Hebrews 4:10).

Lord, give me rest for my body, soul, mind, and spirit. In the name of Jesus, I pray. Amen.

DAY 10

A DAY OF REST CONTINUES
Read Genesis 2:3

Before we get into why rest is important, think of someone famous, someone whose life had a major impact on others. How about Henry Ford, the car manufacturer who produced cars so they could be available for the average person back when only the rich could afford such a luxury? Henry implemented the gift God gave him, and not many people would question his knowledge and authority when it came to cars because he was there from the very beginning.

Yet, when we read what God said about creation, the One who not only witnessed all that took place but caused it all to happen, we have no problem questioning what He tells us. We will soon discover why this is, but for now let's go back to God's creation which took place over the course of seven days, what we know as a week.

Here we are, more than 6,000 years later, and seven days

remains a time marker for one week. When God finished all He had created in six days, when He saw that it was all good, He sanctified the seventh day and made it holy. If the Creator of the world thought it was necessary to rest after all His work, why should we think any differently?

In the not too distant past in America, Sunday was set aside as a day of worship and prayer, a day to spend with family enjoying each other's company and catching up with all the week's activities. Today, it is just another day to many people. There used to be a Blue Law which meant businesses were closed, allowing families an opportunity to go to church. This has changed so drastically that now our society almost considers it weird that places like Hobby Lobby and Chick-fil-a close their doors on Sunday.

Not only do professional sports vie with family and church time on Sunday, but our kids are bombarded with choices in sports, including soccer, football, and basketball to name a few. These activities often require travel away from home on the weekends. When we weigh our options in today's culture, this might be a good teaching opportunity for our kids to show them what is important in our lives and how to balance our commitment to God with the pressures of the world.

The Sabbath Day was so important to the Lord, He included it in the Ten Commandments: "Remember the Sabbath Day to keep it holy." Have we gotten so far away from God that we have forgotten the Sabbath Day to keep it holy? "Return to me," says the Lord Almighty, "and I will return to you," says the Lord Almighty (Zechariah 1:3). Maybe it's time we got back to the things that really matter and put God first in our lives (Matthew 6:33).

Lord, fill my heart with Your presence. Guide me by Your Spirit and give me the ability to be in tune with Your plans and purposes for my life, including taking the time needed to stop working and rest. In the precious name of Jesus, I pray. Amen.

DAY 11

ADAM AND EVE
Read Genesis 2:4-25

Shopping at Walmart is a reminder of how diverse and creative the Lord is. There are young, old, tall, short, fat, thin, long hair, short hair, bald, black, brown, and white shoppers. Each of us is different, yet the same. We all have one head, one nose, one mouth, two ears, two eyes, a neck, a chest, a body, two arms, two hands with ten fingers, two legs, and two feet with ten toes. God is the one who came up with the idea to create man and woman, not the other way around.

The Lord God formed the man from the dust of the ground and breathed into his nostrils the breath of life, and the man became a living being. He was perfect and the Lord God took the man and put him in the Garden of Eden to work it and take care of it. He commanded the man, "You are free to eat from any tree in the garden; but you must not eat from the tree of the knowledge of good and evil, for when you eat of it you will surely die" (Genesis 2:16-17). And then something happened which is up for great debate in our modern world. The Lord God said, "It is not good for the man to be alone. I will make a helper suitable for him" (Genesis 2:18). So the Lord God caused the man to fall into a deep sleep; and while he was sleeping, He took one of the man's ribs and closed up the place with flesh. Then the Lord God made a woman from the rib He had taken out of the man, and He brought her to the man.

Notice how it says "helper," not servant, not slave, not unequal but "helper." The lines are blurred today, to the point where some people question whether they are a man or woman. This may seem sane to some but in reality, it causes a lot of confusion, for it makes us master of our own destiny and takes away from who and what God made us to be. In the book of the prophet Jeremiah, God tells him, "Before I formed you in the womb, I knew you; before you were born I set you apart; I appointed you as a prophet to the nations" (Jeremiah 1:5). This was not only a word for Jeremiah, but it is a word for us. God does not make mistakes. He knew us before we were even formed in the womb and He set us apart to be a holy people for Him (Ephesians 1:4). Though we may not be appointed a prophet to the nations, He knows the plans He has for us, plans to prosper and not to harm, plans to give hope and a future (Jeremiah 29:11).

God knew the plans He had for Adam and Eve. The choice was theirs. Would they remain perfect before the Lord and follow His plan, or would they choose to go their own way apart from Him? Sadly, we know the answer to that. Oh, but the story has not yet ended. It has only begun. We are about to embark on a journey that will make it possible to know the God who spoke and it came to pass; the God who loves us with an everlasting love and draws us to Him with loving-kindness. He is the Lord, the God of all creation. Is there anything too hard for Him? (Isaiah 14:27, 43:13; Jeremiah 32:27).

Lord, Your creation is beyond my understanding. The workings of the human body are a magnificent testimony to Your greatness. Help me to remember that I did not form myself but that it was You who chose to make me in Your image, to Your glory and praise. It is me who chose to go my own way. Bring me back to You, O Lord, that I may know Your greatness once again. In the name of Jesus, I pray. Amen.

DAY 12

THE FALL OF MANKIND
Read Genesis 3:1-6

*N*ow the serpent was more crafty than any of the wild animals the Lord God had made. Apparently, he could speak and Eve was close enough to hear him when he asked, "Did God really say, 'You must not eat from any tree in the garden?'" (Genesis 3:1). Eve responded to the serpent, "We may eat fruit from the trees in the garden but God did say, 'You must not eat fruit from the tree that is in the middle of the garden, and you must not touch it, or you will die'" (Genesis 3:3). Then like the sly devil we know him to be, I imagine him in a snarly, sort of "I know it all" way, saying, "You will not surely die; for God knows that when you eat of it your eyes will be opened and you will be like God, knowing good and evil" (Genesis 3:5).

In other words, who does God think He is? You can decide for yourself what is good and what is evil. This must have sounded pretty plausible. Since Eve likely had been hanging around listening to the serpent for a while, she convinced herself that what he was telling her was true. This time when she looked at the fruit of the tree, it appeared good for food and pleasing to the eye. Because she now believed it was desirable for gaining wisdom, she took some and ate it. Not wanting to be alone in this delectable taste of fruit, she handed it to her husband, who also ate it.

The serpent must have rejoiced, thinking he had outsmarted God, not knowing that God would, in time, give us an entire library of books from which to learn how to get back into relationship with Him. But why was there craftiness in God's perfect creation? Was it a trick to see if Adam and Eve would believe the lie of the serpent? Or was it because of the earlier rebellion in the heavenly realms? Was it to see if Adam and Eve would remain faithful? I do not know, but I do know that God is faithful. He will not let us be tempted beyond what we can bear. But when we are tempted, He will also provide a way out so that we can stand up under it (1 Corinthians 10:13).

When tempted, no one should say, "God is tempting me." For God cannot be tempted by evil, nor does He tempt anyone; but each one is tempted when, by his or her own evil desire, he or she is dragged away and enticed. Then after desire has conceived, it gives birth to sin; and sin when it is full-grown, gives birth to death (James 1:13-15).

It's for certain Eve allowed her desire to become full-grown and she gave in to her temptation. May we learn from her mistake and make every effort to remain faithful to the God who has given us our very breath.

Heavenly Father, Jesus taught us to pray: Do not let us yield to temptation but deliver us from evil. I pray this in His precious name. Amen.

DAY 13

THE CONFRONTATION
Read Genesis 3:7-15

After eating the forbidden fruit, the eyes of Adam and Eve were opened and they saw that they were naked. They sewed fig leaves together making coverings for themselves. Then they heard the sound of the Lord as He walked in the garden in the cool of the day and they hid from the Lord among the trees of the garden. Isn't this just like us, to hide when we know we've done something wrong?

But the Lord called out to Adam, "Where are you?" He answered, "I heard you in the garden and I was afraid because I was naked; so I hid." God said, "Who told you you were naked? Have you eaten from the tree that I commanded you not to eat from?" Adam answered, "The woman You put here with me, she gave me some fruit from the tree and I ate it." (Genesis 3:9-12)

Not only was he blaming someone else for what he did, but he blamed God for the woman whom "You put here with me."

Wow, did he ever set the standard, one which continues to this very day.

Then the Lord said to Eve, "What is this you have done?" She said, "The serpent deceived me, and I ate" (Genesis 3:13). She certainly was a quick learner.

So the Lord said to the serpent, "Because you have done this, cursed are you above all the livestock and wild animals. You will crawl on your belly and you will eat dust all the days of your life. And I will put enmity between you and the woman, and between your offspring and hers; he will crush your head and you will strike his heel" (Genesis 3:14-15).

It's at this time that God reveals that in fact, Satan has not outsmarted God at all. The battle has only begun and Satan is the one who will be crushed.

I sometimes wonder if Adam and Eve had been humble and contrite, coming before the Lord in repentance, asking for forgiveness, would He have given them a second chance? We will never know because the moment rebellion set in, it gained a stronghold that would not be broken until Jesus came to set the captives free (Luke 4:18-19).

Lord, I am only beginning to understand Your unfolding story of creation, rebellion, forgiveness and redemption. If nothing else, open my eyes to see and my ears to hear as You show me what is good and pleasing in Your sight. In the name of Jesus, I pray. Amen.

DAY 14

THE CURSE
Read Genesis 3:16-24

God continued speaking, first to Eve, then to Adam, after which He made garments of skin for them. God killed an animal to make these garments and for the first time, blood was shed because of their sin. Already, Eden felt the pain of disobedience, but it didn't end there.

The Lord said, "The man has now become like one of us, knowing good and evil. He must not be allowed to reach out his hand and take also from the tree of life and eat and live forever."

This must have been something Adam and Eve were contemplating, for God quickly banished them from the Garden of Eden. Instead of having everything provided for them, they now would have to work the ground from which Adam had been taken.

Then God placed on the east side of the garden a cherubim and a flaming sword flashing back and forth to guard the way to the tree of life (Genesis 3:24). There was no way He was going to let them live forever in their sin. Alleluia to that!

Since that sad and sorrowful day, life has never been easy. The perfection, peace, and love that went into making everything God created to be good was gone. Now Adam had to work by the sweat of his brow in order to grow food. Eve would experience great pain as she brought their children into the world. And it wouldn't be long before her two sons, Cain and Abel, grew up and the first recorded murder took place. When sin entered the world, the "genie" was let out of the bottle and there was no way to put it back, but this genie didn't get to grant three wishes. Sin only brought with it rebellion, deceit, and unbelief, the world in which we live today.

Lord, I sometimes wonder how it all happened. How were Adam and Eve so convinced that You lied to them? But then when I consider the world today, things haven't really changed. There seems to be more unbelief than ever. Thank You that You have given me hope not only for now but for the future. In the name of Jesus, I pray. Amen.

DAY 15

CAIN AND ABEL
Read Genesis 4:1-7

Throughout my life, sadly I have too often been quick to dish out criticism, but when it comes to receiving it, my quickness disappears like a turtle hiding its head in its shell. I don't like being on the receiving end. However, criticism can be a good thing when it's meant to help someone be right with God. The Bible says, "Rebuke a wise man and he will love you. Instruct a wise man and he will be wiser still. Teach a righteous man and he will add to his learning" (Proverbs 9:8-9). In the words of Jesus, "Those whom I love I rebuke and discipline. So be earnest and repent" (Revelation 3:19), which brings us to today's study.

It began when Adam knew his wife, Eve. She got pregnant and had a son named Cain. She later gave birth to his brother Abel. As we read the story, we can surmise that Cain and Abel were taught about God and that they were to bring an offering to Him.

In the course of time, Cain brought some of the fruits of the soil as an offering to the Lord, but Abel brought fat portions from some of the firstborn of his flock. The Lord looked with favor on Abel and his offering, but on Cain and his offering he did not look with favor. So Cain was very angry, and his face was downcast (Genesis 4:3-5).

What was wrong with Cain's offering? It was not what God required, and Cain had to have known this. In order to bring the offering God wanted, Cain would have had to ask his brother for it. But that meant humbling himself, which he most likely didn't want to do. He worked hard and wanted to bring the fruit of his own work.

Then the Lord said to Cain, "Why are you angry? Why is your face downcast? If you do what is right, will you not be accepted? But if you do not do what is right, sin is crouching at your door; it desires to have you, but you must master it" (Genesis 4:6-7).

Isn't the Lord so gracious, so kind, even gentle in his criticism? He is asking Cain to think about what he has done and consider the consequences. The choice was his.

How do we measure up in the choices we make each day? Are we trying to do things our way in order to show how great we are, or do we work at whatever we do and do it with all our heart as though working for the Lord, not for men (Colossians 3:23)? The Lord is watching, for He knows the thoughts and intents of our hearts.

Lord, so many times I have fallen short of what I know pleases You. I act and speak before I think and do not always consider others. Help me to listen when You speak, to learn from what You say, and, most importantly, to do what You require. In the precious name of Jesus, I pray. Amen.

DAY 16

ANGER
Read Genesis 4:8-9

*A*nger is a powerful emotion. If left unchecked, it begins to fester like an open wound, until suddenly, like a volcano, it explodes and everything within spews forth, leaving a path of destruction and devastation. Unlike a volcano, though, anger can be controlled if it is plucked from the ground by its roots to wither and die like a weed. This was the choice Cain faced, but like his father before him, he refused God's warning. In turn, he murdered his own brother, whom he should have protected and loved, not hated.

The innocent, the one who had done nothing wrong, suffered at the hand of the guilty, which is a recurring theme throughout the Bible, and even today. Cain set the standard for wickedness, and though anger may not always result in murder, it can destroy the very heart and soul of all who are its target. That's not all it does. When its owner refuses to come clean, pride and arrogance compound its grief.

After Abel's murder, the Lord asked Cain, "Where is your brother Abel?"(Genesis 4:9a). Every time I read this response I cringe at the thought of answering God Almighty in this way, but there it is in black and white for us to read. "I don't know," Cain replied. "Am I my brother's keeper?" (Genesis 4:9b). Even when confronted with his crime by God, who knows all things, he refused to yield. It was as though the anger Cain felt had seeped deep into his very being to the point that no matter what God said to him, he could not or would not take responsibility for his own actions (Proverbs 29:11).

What about us? Do we allow God to search our hearts, minds, and souls? If we do, what is our response when He reveals the truth of our innermost thoughts and desires? Do we become angry, or do we confess our sin and master it (1 John 1:9)? The choice we make has eternal consequences.

O, Lord, forgive me for the times I have allowed anger to well up within me and destroy not only my peace but the peace of those around me. Search my heart, my mind, my soul, and see if there be any evil thought or desire within me. Help me to be honest with You and with myself, knowing that You have given me the strength and power to overcome the enemy of my soul. In the name of Jesus, I pray. Amen.

DAY 17

THE PUNISHMENT
Read Genesis 4:9-24

Having worked in the federal court system for almost 15 years, I've witnessed many defendants take the stand trying to convince a jury that they were innocent of the crimes for which they were charged. I've even heard one or two admit their guilt, then try and finagle their way out by justifying what they did. The thing that struck me the most was their lack of shame or remorse. Their only concern was to somehow get away with their crime and avoid any form of punishment.

It's not the first time this has happened; nor will it be the last. It actually began in Chapter 4 of Genesis when God confronted Cain with the murder of his brother and then pronounced judgment on him. Cain's only concern was that his punishment was more than he could bear. Without any hint of remorse for killing his brother, He said to the Lord, "Today you are driving me out from the land and I will be hidden from Your presence. I will be a restless wanderer on the earth, and whoever finds me will kill me" (Genesis 4:13-14). Once again, God, who is rich in mercy (Ephesians 2:4), did not exact on Cain what in my way of thinking Cain justly deserved. Instead, He said to Cain, "Not so. If anyone kills Cain, he will suffer vengeance seven times over." Then the Lord put a mark on Cain so that no one who found him would kill him (Genesis 4:15).

So Cain went out from the Lord's presence and lived apart from God in the land of Nod, east of Eden (Genesis 4:16). Life continued for Cain. He married, had a son, built a city and named it after his son. A secular society apart from God emerged, though we don't know anything about Cain's descendants until we come to a man named Lamech, who married two women. He is the first man we know who defied God's design of one man and one woman in marriage. He too killed a man and then boasted about it to his wives, "I have killed a man for wounding me, a young man for injuring me. If Cain is avenged seven times, then Lamech 70 times seven." There is no sign of remorse, only a boastful proudness that says, "If Cain got away with it, so can I."

But Cain did not get away with anything. His legacy has been handed down through the ages. If we listen carefully to some of those who have committed crimes or evil acts, they themselves cry, "victim," and, like Cain, refuse to admit any culpability. However, God sees and knows everything. One day we must all appear before the judgment seat of Christ, that each one may receive what is due him for the things done while in the body, whether good or bad (2 Corinthians 5:10).

Lord, forgive me for the times I have tried to get away with sin, thinking I could hide it from You. Your word tells us there is no place to hide from Your presence. Help me to be careful and do that which is pleasing in Your sight, that which honors You and puts me in a right relationship with You, Lord of lords and King of kings. In the name of Jesus, I pray. Amen.

DAY 18

HOPE IS NOT LOST
Read Genesis 4:25-26

Adam and Eve had another son named Seth. Seth later had a son named Enosh. "At that time, men began to call on the name of the Lord" (Genesis 4:26). What a blessed statement of hope that is.

Though we have no clue how many children Adam and Eve actually had, we know they had Cain, Abel and Seth. Cain chose the way of the world; Seth, the way of the Lord. This is our real choice in life. It is not about race (there is only one, the human race), or religion (there are so many, it's hard to count) or sexual orientation (God created man and woman). It's about which path we choose.

Jesus said in Matthew 7:13, "Enter through the narrow gate. For wide is the gate and broad is the road that leads to destruction, and many enter through it. But small is the gate and narrow the road that leads to life, and only a few find it."

When I began this Old Testament study, I did not attribute

such significance to Cain's actions. I've read it many times, not thinking this is the actual broad road of which Jesus spoke, the one that leads to destruction. However, it is indeed the path that's all about "me, me, me," and any benefits derived from my efforts are attributed to "me." The way of Seth is the path of righteousness which leads to a relationship with Jesus. We are not told that this is an easy path. As a matter of fact, the way of righteousness isn't easy. It is something we must want and desire above all else.

Scripture tells us to seek the Lord with all of our hearts and we will find Him, call on Him while He is near (Isaiah 55:6). "You will seek me and find me when you seek Me with all of your heart. I will be found by you," declares the Lord (Jeremiah 29:13). It is worth the effort, for in the end, we reap the benefits of God's promises, spending eternity in His presence.

Lord, when You spoke, Moses listened and wrote, and today we are all reaping the benefits of his choice to follow You with all his heart. Thank You for Your word that guides me into Your truth. Help me to make wise choices that honor You and bring peace and freedom to my life. In the name of Jesus, I pray. Amen.

DAY 19

MALE AND FEMALE
Read Genesis 5:1-2

When God created man, He made him in His own image. He created them male and female and blessed them. When they were created, He called them "man" (Genesis 5:1). Today's society is obsessed with gender, and this Scripture may cause those who disagree with it, or find it offensive, to squirm like a worm on a fish hook. It also may be one of the reasons why scientists and philosophers alike try to discredit not only this Scripture, but the entire book of Genesis. If their efforts are successful, and they are making great strides, the remainder of the Bible can be tossed aside on the trash heap of history and now we can make our own rules.

When I was growing up, referring to a group of people that included women as "men" was not offensive. Never would my generation have believed that when we were to be in our sixties and seventies men could say they are "women," and women could say they are "men," and those who disagree with them are labeled as "hate-filled homophobes who live in the dark ages."

I've considered not addressing this subject at all, but in today's age of same-sex legalized marriage, homosexuals adopting children, couples keeping the gender of their children secret and calling them "theybies," and a father being court-ordered not to call his son a boy, it is something that cannot be ignored. It truly is attacking the very essence of who God made each and every one of us to be.

If we do not know who we are, then who are we? It's interesting that a man can now say he's a woman and vice versa, but why must a man or woman, who thinks they are not a man or woman, limit themselves to being the other gender? Why can't they be an animal or plant, or anything else they want to be? I say this with all sincerity, not to poke fun or make a joke. To not know who we are brings nothing but confusion, and God is not the author of confusion (1 Corinthians 14:33, KJV).

If I am being politically incorrect, I make no apologies for believing what God said in Genesis 5:2. It comes down to what the Bible is all about: Will we be who God has chosen and ordained us to be, or will we choose our own way?

Lord, in the book of Jeremiah, You told him, "Before I formed you in the womb I knew you, before you were born I set you apart. I appointed you as a prophet to the nations." You also say in 2 Timothy 3:16 that all Scripture is God-breathed and useful for teaching, rebuking, correcting, and training in righteousness. May each and every one who seeks You come to know and understand that what You said to Jeremiah is true for all of us; that You knew us before we were even born, You knew whether we would be male or female, and You have a plan and purpose for our lives. In the precious name of Jesus, I pray. Amen.

DAY 20

FROM ADAM TO NOAH
Read Genesis 5:3-32

From Adam came Seth, Enosh, Kenan, Mahalel, Jared, and Enoch, who became the father of Methuselah. Enoch walked with God for 300 years and had other sons and daughters. He lived 365 years and walked with God; then he was no more, because God took him away (Genesis 5:22-24).

Amidst the evil and sin which existed in the world, its effect did not taint the line of Seth. If anything, the knowledge of God was handed down in such a way that one man, Enoch, was righteous enough to pass over from life on earth to heaven without physically dying. We are not told much else about Enoch except that he was faithful (Hebrews 11:5) and that he prophesied about evil men (Jude 14-16). Is it possible his words were so despised that God took him before he too was murdered? Perhaps, but only God knows the answer to that question.

Enoch named his son Methuselah (Genesis 5:21). If we've ever wondered whether names have a meaning, and if God puts it on the hearts of the parents what to name their children, Methuselah is such an example. His name means "when he dies, it shall be sent." If that name sounds familiar, it may be because you've heard the saying, "He's as old as Methuselah," who lived 969 years—longer than any human being who has ever lived.

What does it mean "when he dies, it shall be sent"? Methuselah was the father of Lamech (a different Lamech than the line of Cain), and Lamech was the father of Noah, who was the father of Shem, Ham, and Japheth. When Methuselah died, the flood came, and, oh, what a flood it was!

Lord, thank You for our rich heritage from the beginning of creation. We have been adopted into Your family as Your sons and daughters through Jesus Christ, Your Son. Because of Your word, we know the lineage of Jesus to which we belong.

Help me live in the heritage You have given me and help me teach my children so they may teach their children. Who knows that one day, they may walk with You and be no more because they have crossed over from this life into eternity. In the name of Jesus, I pray. Amen.

DAY 21

THE FLOOD
Read Genesis 6:1-8:17

*I*f you're ever in or near Williamstown, Kentucky, be sure and stop at the Ark Encounter, a life-size reconstruction of Noah's Ark. This massive structure, which housed Noah and his family, as well as pairs of all creatures that have the breath of life in them, gives us an inkling of what it must have been like during the flood that wiped every living thing off the face of the earth. There is enough information contained in this one place to assuage the doubts of even the most ardent unbelievers.

The flood for which this ark was built took place after people began to increase in number on the earth and evil abounded. The Lord saw how great man's wickedness was and that every inclination of the thoughts of their hearts was only evil, all the time. The Lord was grieved that He made man on the earth, and His heart was filled with pain (Genesis 6:6).

To think of God feeling pain in His heart for having created human beings stops me dead in my tracks. Have you ever felt that kind of pain from being deeply hurt? If so, it is the type of pain that has no cure. It can't be surgically cut out or made better with a Band-Aid. It's a pain that brings a waterfall of tears. However, there was one man who was righteous and blameless among the people of his time. His name was Noah and he walked with God, who instructed him to build an ark. Once finished, God sent two of every kind of animal to board the ark and God shut them all in. The floodwaters began covering the entire earth with water and every living thing that moved on the earth perished (Genesis 7:21-23).

God was saying to Noah, "You have been faithful and obedient, and I'm going to begin anew with you," a forerunner of Christ's salvation (Acts 4:12; 13:46-48). The flood is like baptism, for when we were baptized into Christ Jesus we were baptized into his death. Therefore, we were buried with Him through baptism into death in order that, just as Christ was raised from the dead, through the glory of the Father, we too may now live a new life (Romans 6:1-11).

Then God said to Noah, "Come out of the ark (your old way of life)... Bring out every kind of living creature that is with you...so that they can multiply on the earth and be fruitful and increase in number" (Genesis 8:17). Such was Jesus's command to His disciples, "Therefore, go and make disciples of all nations, baptizing them in the name of the Father and of the Son and of the Holy Spirit, teaching them to obey everything I have commanded you" (Matthew 28:19-20).

Lord, may my life be transformed by the renewing of my mind, putting away my former way of life, in order that I may be able to test and approve what Your will is—Your good, pleasing, and perfect will, for the new life I now live. In the name of Jesus, I pray. Amen.

DAY 22

PUTTING GOD FIRST
Read Genesis 8:18-22

There's not much question fresh air and sunshine would have been welcomed after weeks and weeks of being cooped up in the ark with smelly, noisy animals. Stepping onto dry land must have been a funny feeling after riding the waves of the flood. Noah didn't waste much time in honoring God for bringing them through the storm. One of the first things he did was build an altar to the Lord, upon which he made a burnt offering sacrifice of clean animals and birds. The Lord smelled the pleasing aroma and said in His heart, "Never again will I curse the ground because of man, even though every inclination of his heart is evil from childhood" (Genesis 8:21).

Though the smell of the sacrificial animals and birds may have been pungent to Noah, to God it was a pleasing aroma, just as Christ who loved us and gave Himself up for us was a fragrant offering and sacrifice to God (Ephesians 5:2).

The people of the earth had become so wicked that God

destroyed them by flooding the entire earth. Now He vows to never destroy them by flood again, even though "every inclination of man's heart is evil from childhood" (Genesis 8:21). Was the blood sacrifice of animals by Noah an atonement for the sins of mankind, perhaps bringing about this change from God? I'm not certain of the answer, but I do know animals were killed in the Garden of Eden because of sin (Genesis 3:21) and Abel offered the fat portions from some of his firstborn of his flock to the Lord (Genesis 4:2-4). After Christ came into the world, He said, "Sacrifice and offering you did not desire but a body you prepared for me; with burnt offerings and sin offerings you were not pleased...but I, O God, have come to do your will." And by that will, we have been made holy through the sacrifice of the body of Jesus Christ once for all (Hebrews 10:4-10).

Noah obeyed God by putting Him first in his life. His obedience made it possible for the human race to continue and Christ's obedience on the cross made it possible for us to be put back into a right relationship with our Creator (Romans 5:11).

Lord, help me, as Noah did, to put You first in my life, setting aside all the things which constantly vie for my attention. Help me also to remember the sacrifice which Jesus made for me by shedding His blood for my sins. In whose holy name, I pray. Amen.

DAY 23

A NEW COVENANT WITH A SIGN
Read Genesis 9:1-17

God blessed Noah and his sons, saying to them, "Be fruitful and increase in number and fill the earth," the same words which He earlier spoke to Adam (Genesis 1:28). It was a new beginning for Noah and his family, although some things would be different. Before the flood, animals were not fearful of people, but now they would be; and everything that lived and moved would now be food to eat, except for meat that has its lifeblood still in it (Genesis 9:2-5).

The Lord gave Noah instructions on how to set up a system of government, which included giving an accounting when one man killed another. Unlike Cain and Lamech, who were not put to death for their murders, God told Noah, "Whoever sheds the blood of man, by man shall his blood be shed; for in the image of God has God made man" (Genesis 9:6). Now, if someone were found guilty of murder, their own life would be forfeited. God also said to Noah that this punishment would be meted out by man, not by God.

These changes indicate that though the flood destroyed everyone and everything that was not in the ark, sin had not been eradicated from the earth. It was a new beginning and these were God's instructions on how to get started afresh.

Then God said to Noah, "I have set my rainbow in the clouds...This is the sign of the covenant I have established between Me and all life on earth" (Genesis 9:13). Years ago, when I lived in Virginia, there was a horrific storm with high winds and downpours of rain, leaving debris scattered everywhere. After it was over, a brilliant double rainbow lit up the sky. It was so astonishing, it made the nightly news. Looking out my bedroom window at this beautiful sight, I thought back to God's promise and was thankful that though we too experience the storms of life, the rainbow that follows reminds us that God's promises are true and that this covenant will remain until there are a new heaven and a new earth. The first heaven and earth will pass away...And the dwelling of God will be with men and He will live with them. They will be His people and God Himself will be with them and be their God" (Revelation 21:1-3).

Lord, I ask that You keep me in covenant with You all the days of my life, remembering that after every storm there is a rainbow. In the name of Jesus, I pray. Amen.

DAY 24

NO RESTRAINT
Read Genesis 9:18-21

After the waters receded and life began to settle down, Noah began to till the soil. He planted a vineyard and made it into wine. When he drank some of it, he got drunk (Genesis 9:21). Noah, a man who was righteous and blameless before God, who had probably preached many a sermon while building the ark. How did he allow this to happen? The answer: God destroyed everything with the flood, except sin. Sin is so real, it can cause even the best of men to do wrong when they forget that it is only by God's grace we are able to overcome.

Not only did Noah get drunk, but he laid uncovered inside his tent. The word "uncovered" in the Hebrew language as used here describes a very definitive act with implications of sexual perversion. So it wasn't just a matter of getting drunk and being naked. The sad thing is, despite all the good things Noah did, this is the one thing mentioned about him after the flood that was not good, and its implications are still felt to this day.

We have restraints in life that are instilled in us at a young age, from sources such as our upbringing, our conscience, laws enacted by the state, or any number of things. Take away the restraints, and we discover what we are really like, and this easily happens when things like alcohol and drugs are abused.

For it is by grace that we have been saved, through faith, and this is not from ourselves; it is the gift of God, not by works, so that no one can boast (Ephesians 2:8). True restraint comes by the grace of God. Perhaps Noah got carried away and thought his accomplishments were of his own making, but for whatever reason, he strayed away from his first love. We don't know much else about him after the flood.

What we can learn from this is that we are all sinners, even righteous Noah. If we claim to be without sin, we deceive ourselves and the truth is not in us. But if we confess our sins, the Lord is faithful and just and will forgive us our sins and purify us from all unrighteousness (1 John 1:8-9).

Lord, I pray I never forget that it is by Your grace that I have been saved from the ravages of sin. Help me not to be tempted by the ways of this world, which continually entice me to turn from You. I ask for Your strength to fight the good fight in order to remain holy and righteous in Your sight. In the name of Jesus, I pray. Amen.

DAY 25

GAZING AND GOSSIPING
Read Genesis 9:22-23

What came next in the unfolding events of life after the flood is Ham, who would become the father of Canaan, saw his father's nakedness and told his two brothers who were outside the tent (Genesis 9:22). The sin here is not necessarily that Ham saw his father naked, but that he did nothing about it. Instead, he gazed at his father, which meant he lingered and looked long and hard at him. Then he went out of the tent and told his brothers what he had seen, maybe even with a little bravado as he gossiped about his own father.

Shem was appalled by this and enlisted the help of his brother Japheth by taking a garment and laying it across their shoulders. Then they walked into the tent backward and covered their father's nakedness without turning to look at him (9:23).

The Bible says to flee temptation (2 Timothy 2:22-26), which means to do an about-face as though you had run into a brick wall. Turn around and run as fast as your feet will carry you, run into the arms of Jesus, the One who gives us the strength and ability to do all things through Him (Philippians 4:13). If we can grasp this concept – that we are unable to do life on our own – and take hold of Jesus like we would a life preserver, as though we will never let go, we will endure to the end (Matthew 24:13). Whether it's until our death, or meeting Him in the air when He returns, we will endure. We are overcomers through the One in whom we live and move and have our very being (Acts 17:28).

Ham's choice was to go his own way, and the result of his actions trickles down throughout the entirety of the Old Testament, which we will read about time and again. On the other hand, let's not forget Shem and Japheth, who chose God's way and through one of them came the Savior of the world (Luke 3:35).

Lord, I cannot thank You enough for giving us Your story, of revealing to us how the mystery of life has unfolded before our very eyes. You have given the history of creation and gone all the way to the future - to the end of the world. What a blessed generation we are, to have it all written down in one book to read over and over again. May I hide Your word in my heart so that I will not sin against You. In the name of Jesus, I pray. Amen.

DAY 26

CURSED AGAIN
Read Genesis 9:24-25

Noah was pretty upset when he awoke from his wine and discovered what Ham did, so much so he said, "Cursed be Canaan! The lowest of slaves will he be to his brothers" (Genesis 9:25). While we may be inclined to think this was some angry old man who was upset that his son had seen him naked and gossiped to his brothers about it, it is much more than that. What Noah saw in his son was the wretchedness that would take place in the years to come and spread all throughout history. He saw his own weakness in his son and the heredity which would be passed down the line to future generations.

What Noah prophesied came true. Ham was the father of Canaan, which became the nation that inhabited the land that later was given to the twelve tribes of Israel called the Promised Land. The Canaanites became so evil that God ultimately removed them from the land and cities they inhabited, and gave the land to His own people, the people of Israel (Deuteronomy 9:4-5).

These are not just words written on a page to read for our enjoyment. They are the truth of God which continually reveals the two choices, the two lines, which exist in life: God's way, or our own way. The way of Ham, as the way of Cain, leads to the wide path of destruction which Jesus spoke of; the way of Shem, the way of Seth, is the narrow path which ultimately leads to life everlasting.

Lord, at this point I am without words to even write as I am overwhelmed with the cohesiveness of Your revelation through Your Word. Teach me Your ways, instill in me Your righteousness, that I may choose the way of Shem, the way of Jesus, the way of everlasting life with You. In the holy name of Jesus, I pray. Amen.

DAY 27

THE BLESSING
Read Genesis 9:26-28

Noah also saw the righteousness of his other two sons before the flood. He blessed them, for they had shown respect to their father by covering up his nakedness and refusing to look upon him. Noah's prophecies about them also came true. We know through Noah's blessings that Shem was in relationship with God and would continue to be so through the generations. Shem not only served the Lord, but we know by the documented genealogies that his descendants are the Jews, from whom came Jesus, the Savior of the world (Luke 3:21-27; John 3:16-18). Japheth as well was blessed for his willingness to follow his brother's lead by respecting his father and not looking upon his nakedness; thereby sharing in Shem's blessing.

When I began this study of the Old Testament, I had no idea the significance of these events and their importance, even though I've read them a number of times. If you are not yet getting that flavor of all of this, and its implications on our lives, please do not give up. There is so much more we have to learn about what follows from these events. We are only in Chapter 9 of Genesis. There are 41 more chapters and 38 more Old Testament books. They reveal the entirety of God's story, the magnificence of His creation, and the mystery of His ways.

The love, mercy, and grace that He extends to us are beyond our comprehension because He alone is God, and there is none other; apart from Him, there is no God (Isaiah 45:5). Is there any God besides Him? No, there is no other Rock that He knows of, not one (Isaiah 44:8). This is what the Lord says, Your Redeemer, who formed you in the womb, "I am the Lord who has made all things, who alone stretched out the heavens, who spread out the earth by Myself..." (Isaiah 44:24). What an awesome God. We can know Him and we can pray to Him. He hears us and listens to us and knows our every need before we even ask (Matthew 6:8).

Lord, when I consider Your heavens and the work of Your hands, I am in awe that You love me, that You care about my life, and that You have a plan and purpose for it. I pray that we will all come to know the incomparable power of Your riches and the blessings You have promised from before the creation of the world so that we may come to know You and serve You in a real and personal way. In the name of Jesus, I pray. Amen.

DAY 28

BE FRUITFUL AND FILL THE EARTH
Read Genesis 9:29-10:32

Noah lived to be 950 years. That is not something we can comprehend. If someone lives to be 100 years or older today, it's newsworthy. We don't know if Noah and his wife had more children after the flood. If they did, they are not accounted for in the genealogy. But even if they didn't, Noah's three sons did. That must have been a daunting thing, coming out of the ark, realizing that there were only eight people on the entire earth, and they were the ones responsible for repopulation! Japheth had seven sons, Ham had four sons, and Shem had five sons. From these six people came many more sons and daughters, some of whom became nations. From Japheth came the maritime peoples who spread out into their territories by their clans with their nations. From Ham came Nimrod, who grew to be a mighty warrior on the earth and established a kingdom from which some of the first cities came. He built Nineveh, a place which is referred to later in the Old Testament.

From Ham came the Canaanite people, who will be mentioned many times throughout the Old Testament as being at odds with those who become God's chosen people, who are the descendants of Shem.

One of Shem's sons was named Eber, which came from the Hebrew verb "abar," meaning, "to cross over" or "to pass through." From Eber comes the word "Hebrew."[1] The Hebrews are the Jews, the chosen people of God, and around whom the majority and remainder of the Bible focus.

These are the clans of Noah's sons, according to their lines of descent, within their nations. From these clans, the nations spread out over the earth after the flood, and from Noah and his three sons descended all peoples of the earth.

Lord, You and You alone know my beginning and my ending. I am not my own, though I often think I am. Some people are proud of their heritage and ancestry; still others have no knowledge of theirs. No matter a person's family history, Lord, help me remember that I belong to You. In the name of Jesus, I pray. Amen.

DAY 29

THE SPOKEN WORD
Read Genesis 11:1-9

*L*anguage. The words we speak and how we communicate with one another. Of all God's creation, humans are the only ones who do this. According to *Ethnologue*, as of April 2020, there are about 7,111 languages spoken around the entire world, but that doesn't include the different dialects.[1]

I love languages and wish I could speak them all, but that would be impossible. I've tried for years to learn and speak Spanish, only getting the very basics, but not enough to communicate effectively. When I went to Germany, I learned enough German to only ask questions. Fortunately, I had a friend with me who knew the language well and was able to help me when the questions were responded to so rapidly. There are times I've wondered where all these languages come from, and then I looked to Scripture and found the answer.

There was a time when the whole earth had a common language and one speech. As all the people came together, they decided to build a tower to heaven so they could make a name for themselves and not be scattered over the face of the earth. Isn't it interesting that the very thing they wanted to accomplish, God quickly put to an end? Their desire was to make a name for themselves, which sounds much like what's happening in our world today. Fame and fortune are the two things most sought after.

The Lord confused their languages so they could not understand each other and scattered them over all the earth. In turn, they stopped building the tower. In the movie, *The Bible,* there is a scene depicting the Tower of Babel. It is mass confusion as people are running in all directions, like chickens trying to find their roost. Eventually, small groups joined together and began wandering off in different directions, never again to be one people with a common language.

There was so much power when the people all spoke one language that the Lord said they could accomplish anything. Because of this, He also said, "Come, let us go down and confuse their language so they will not understand each other," thus, the division among the people of the earth (Genesis 11:7).

But the one who unites him or herself with Jesus becomes one with Him in spirit (1 Corinthians 6:17). It is in this spirit of unity, which brings honor to God, that we once again speak the same language and become, as Jesus prayed, one with the Father, Son, and Holy Spirit.

Heavenly Father, give me wisdom this day to think before I speak and to use my language effectively to lift others up. In the name of Jesus, I pray. Amen.

DAY 30

A RICH HERITAGE
Read Genesis 11:10-26

My mom has a passion for genealogy. She has not only discovered previously unknown things about our family, she traced her side of the family back to William Brewster who came to America on the Mayflower. She spent hours going through records and getting documentation to prove this. I was so excited about it, I applied to the General Society of Mayflower Descendants to become a member, which was easy because my mom did all the work. It was humbling to learn that one of our ancestors actually survived that arduous journey across the open seas.

My mom also told me we had ancestors who came from Kentucky, so when she and my aunt visited us in Tennessee, we took a couple of days to drive there and check it out. Sure enough, we found them at the County Clerk's office. It's pretty exciting to go to a courthouse, or someplace where records are kept, and see the names of your ancestors and information about who they were married to, where they lived and what property they owned. It's like discovering a new part of yourself, which is the way I felt when I began reading Matthew, the first book of the New Testament.

The very first chapter begins with the genealogy of Jesus Christ, going all the way back to Abraham, who we will read about in the 11th chapter of Genesis. As I studied and even memorized Christ's genealogy, I went back to the Old Testament and found the names of all those referred to in Jesus' genealogy. They all existed, and it all began with Abraham who was appointed by God to be the father of a chosen people (the Jews). By Abraham, all the nations of the world would be blessed. Because of Abraham's faithfulness, we have a rich heritage (Romans 8:16-17) when we become followers of Jesus Christ (John 1:12-13).

Thank You, Heavenly Father, for sending Jesus, Who, because of His death and resurrection, gave me a new life by Your Spirit, making me Your child. Watch over me as a parent watches their child. Help me to love and obey You. In the name of Jesus, I pray. Amen.

DAY 31

THE CALL TO CANAAN
Read Genesis 11:27-32

Searching through God's word is like looking for precious gems and metals, even oil, none of which are found on the earth's surface. In order to reap the benefits which they provide, an arduous process of mining and digging has to take place. First, to find these products. Secondly, to harvest them. Then ultimately, prepare them for their intended use. When we dig deep into the Bible, there are many precious gems waiting to be discovered, but it takes time, along with a strong desire to find them (1 Chronicles 28:9). One of those gems is Abram (later named Abraham), who I mentioned yesterday. He was the son of Terah, whose genealogy goes back to Shem, the son of Noah. This genealogy is important because it takes us all the way back to Adam (Luke 3:23-38).

God spoke to Abram saying, "Leave your country, your people and your father's household and go to the land I will show you. I will make you into a great nation and I will bless you… I will bless those who bless you, and whoever curses you I will curse; and all peoples on earth will be blessed through you." And he went, bringing with him his family, his nephew Lot and his father Terah (Genesis 12:1-3).

On the way from Ur (where God called Abram from), Terah wanted to stop in Haran, halfway between Ur and Canaan (where God called Abram to go), and they settled there. We're not told why. Perhaps Terah became sentimental because the name of this town was the same as another one of his sons named Haran (Lot's father) who died. Or perhaps it was because it was the end of the known Chaldean civilization with all of its modern amenities and going any further was going into the unknown. No matter the reason, this wasn't where God intended Abram to stop and put down his roots.

Isn't this what sometimes happens to us as Christians? We ask Jesus to become our Savior, leaving our past life behind, yet, for whatever reason, we don't nurture our relationship with Him and take the time necessary to dig deep into God's word. We keep ourselves from discovering the incomparable great riches He has in store for us, even here on earth (Ephesians 2:6-7).

All during their time in Haran, we have no mention of God speaking to Abram. It wasn't until he was 75 years old, after his father died, that Abram continued the journey to Canaan. It was then that God appeared to him and said, "To your offspring, I will give this land."

At times, we might wonder why we don't hear from the Lord. Could it be that we are stuck in Haran, after He told us to go to Canaan? If so, why do we think He would give us further guidance if we have not even traveled the distance He has told us to go? It wasn't until Abram took the next step and reached his destination that God once again began to speak to him.

Lord, may I answer when You call, and may I journey to the destination You have chosen when You call me to go. In the name of Jesus, I pray. Amen.

DAY 32

MAKING IT RIGHT
Read Genesis 12:1-10

TV news is notorious for reporting bad and often sad news stories, so much so I rarely watch it except to check the local weather. Even our conversations gravitate to negative things, that which is wrong in our world, often making us worry. It's actually rare to hear good news stories or to find solutions for things that are wrong and to make them right.

As Christians, we know what is wrong with our world and we also know how to make it right. We know that salvation is found in no one else other than Jesus, for "there is no other name under heaven given to men by which we must be saved" (Acts 4:12). Yet when a Christian offers that solution, they are often met with resistance, even anger; sometimes called all sorts of names like racist, homophobic, or bigot. To those hearing the salvation message, it's like yelling, "Fire!" in a crowded theater. All they want to do is run away as fast and as far as they can, not realizing a real and personal relationship with Jesus is what makes life right.

They prefer to live life on their own terms, often to their detriment, rather than hear the one true solution that will set them free from the sin that so easily entangles them (Hebrews 12:1). Isn't it odd how that which really is the answer is rejected as foolishness by most people on earth?

Perhaps that's how it was in the days leading up to Abram. Before God chose him, there are only a few people mentioned in the first 11 chapters of the Bible as believing in God, but when we get to the 12th chapter and beyond, the focus changes from many peoples and languages to just one man named Abram, whose faith in God was credited to him as righteousness (Romans 4:1-5). As we will discover, he not only became the father of all nations who were and are blessed because of him, he is also known as a friend of God (James 2:23).

So, from Adam bringing sin into the world, to the flood, and up to the confounding of languages and all the things that were wrong with the world, the focus now turns to one man through whom God's plan of redemption begins. From this point forward is the salvation message telling people how to put things right with God.

Lord, open my heart to Your message. Give me Your understanding and wisdom so that I too may do my part in making things right. In the name of Jesus, I pray. Amen.

DAY 33

TO EGYPT AND BACK
Read Genesis 12:10-20

Abram arrived in Canaan and God told him, "To your offspring, I will give this land" (Genesis 12:1). At the time, Sarai, his wife, was barren and he might have wondered how that was going to happen. Then Abram built an altar to the Lord when he arrived, but apparently he wasn't quite ready to receive wholeheartedly the plan God had in store. For when he saw the land was inhabited and there was a famine, he headed toward Egypt, rather than the land of Canaan. And when he got there, he was afraid for his life and conspired with Sarai to tell Pharaoh they were brother and sister, which was half true, but still a lie.

While in Egypt, Abram acquired a large amount of livestock, as well as camels, menservants, and maidservants. But trouble was brewing in Pharaoh's palace because of Sarai, whom Pharaoh had taken into his harem. When Pharaoh discovered the truth, he was furious and confronted Abram, "What have you done to me? Why didn't you tell me Sarai was your wife? Here now is your wife. Take her and go" (Genesis 12:18-19).

Abram left Pharaoh, then wandered from place to place until he came to a place between Bethel and Ai. He had been there earlier, as it was where he first built an altar to the Lord. It was there that Abram again called on the name of the Lord.

Isn't it interesting that we have no account of God speaking to Abram while in Egypt, but He did speak to Pharaoh. When Pharaoh discovered the truth, he counted himself more righteous than Abram, who left in disgrace. However, Abram returned to the place where he came from and called on the name of the Lord. We know God answered him because this is not the end. It's actually just the beginning, for Abram was getting closer to where God wanted him to be.

The Lord isn't looking for perfection in His people. None exists, except in Christ (Hebrews 7:28). We will read this time and time again throughout the Old and New Testaments. We all have faults, but when we come to the place of repentance, He forgives our sins and looks past those faults, bringing us into communion with Him (1 John 1:9). This is what Abram did, and God restored him.

Lord, help me come back to You when I wander off. Forgive me, heal me and restore me to You, in Jesus' name, I pray. Amen.

DAY 34

UR, HARAN, AND CANAAN

I sought the Lord, and He answered me; He delivered me from all my fears.
Psalm 34:4

Reading about places like Ur, Haran, Canaan, and far away countries like Egypt, you might be asking, "What significance do these places have to me today?" Though these may be physical towns and countries on a map, they are much more than that when we consider what they represent. Ur was Abram's hometown. He grew up there. Everything and everyone he knew was there. He was familiar with his surroundings and was comfortable, yet God called him to leave this place, which he did.

How about you? Are you in a comfortable place right now, everything is going well and you might even be thinking you don't need God's help very much because you are able to take care of things yourself? Is there a tug at your heart that God is calling you to something deeper, something beyond yourself? Is He asking you to get up and follow Him? Are you willing, or would you rather enjoy your comforts and stay where you are?

Haran is the place where Abram settled for a time because his father did not want to travel any further. This is not where God told Abram to settle, but he listened to his dad and stayed there. What about you? Do you allow the wants and desires of others to overrule that which God has called you to? Are you content to be in a place where others want you, missing out on hearing from God because you are not where He wants you to be?

Then there's Canaan, the Promised Land, the place where the Lord appeared to Abram and said, "To your offspring, I will give this land." Abram built an altar there to the Lord. Later, in Bethel, he built another altar to the Lord and called upon His Name. As Abram got closer, he realized it wasn't going to be handed to him on a silver platter. He saw that the land was occupied by others and there was even a severe famine. As we read yesterday, he went to Egypt, a place unaffected by the famine, a place of wealth and prosperity. There is no indication he prayed about this decision, and as we read the events more closely, we discover something else happened. As Abram got closer to Egypt he feared for his life, even asking his wife Sarai to tell Pharaoh she was his sister instead of his wife. He went so far as to put others in jeopardy to save his own skin, which she agreed to go along with.

Abram prospered greatly while in Egypt, but when Pharaoh discovered the truth, he banished Abram from Egypt, and he left in disgrace. This might be a good time to ask yourself, "Am I being totally honest and upright about everything in my life? Or have I allowed my own desires and ambitions to take precedence over what God is saying to me, putting not only myself in jeopardy but others?"

The wonderful thing is that Abram realized the errors of his ways and returned to Canaan, the place where God had called him—the place where he first built an altar. There, Abram called on the name of the Lord. This is where all of us should strive to be, the place where God wants us, the place where He guides us by the gentleness of His Spirit, and we have no fear because He is with us (Psalm 34:4).

Lord, bring me to the place where You want me to be and keep me from wandering, especially when times are rough. In the name of Jesus, I pray. Amen.

DAY 35

ABRAM AND LOT SEPARATE
Read Genesis 13

The things we acquire on our own don't benefit us much when it comes to trusting the Lord. I've found that life goes much better when I allow Him to provide for me. This is why both Abram and Lot should have left behind all they had gained in Egypt, a place they most likely should never have gone to, but they didn't do that. Instead, they brought all their wealth and slaves with them. When they arrived back in Canaan, their possessions caused quarreling and dissension between their herdsmen because there wasn't enough land to support them if they all stayed together (Genesis 13:6-7).

This quarreling left them vulnerable to the Canaanites and Perizzites who were also living in the land at the time. If they couldn't be in agreement among themselves, how would they be strong enough to ward off any attacks from their enemies?

So Abram said to Lot, "Let's not have any quarreling, for we are brothers. Let's part company. If you go to the left, I'll go to the right. If you go to the right, I'll go to the left." Lot saw that the whole plain of Jordan was well watered like the garden of the Lord, and that's what he chose. He wanted what he thought was the best of the land, and he took it (Genesis 13:8-12).

For the first time since leaving Ur, Abram was where the Lord wanted him, away from his family and all to Himself. The Lord said to Abram, "Lift up your eyes from where you are; look north, south, east and west. All the land you see I will give to you and your offspring forever. I will make your offspring like the dust of the earth...Go, walk through the length and breadth of the land, for I am giving it to you." So Abram moved his tents and went to live near the great trees of Mamre at Hebron, where he built an altar to the Lord (Genesis 13:14-18).

Family is one of the strongest bonds we have. It is not easy to let go of those we love, but when it interferes with God's plan for us, we sometimes have to make a choice. It wasn't easy for Abraham, but he did it, and we can too.

Lord, I have often leaned on my own strength and understanding to gain what I thought was necessary to my own wellbeing. Forgive me for not looking to You as the source of my provision. Help me to do better each day and trust You for all my needs. You know what they are even before I ask. In the name of Jesus, I pray. Amen.

DAY 36

ABRAM RESCUES LOT
Read Genesis 14:1-24

Time passed after Abram and Lot went their separate ways. Life was going well for Abram, but down in the fertile valley, trouble was brewing. Rebellion was in the air in Sodom and the surrounding cities, all controlled by chiefs and kings. When those kings got wind of the rebellion, they banded together and pounced on the rebellious people like a lion overtaking its prey. This was the first recorded war in the Bible. Not only did the kings take the goods from these cities, but all the people were hauled away, including Lot and his family (Genesis 14:11-12).

When Abram got the news, he didn't sit back and say, "Well, look at old Lot, he got what he deserved. Why should I do anything to help him?" No. His first thoughts were not of himself, but of his nephew and family who were taken prisoner and carted away from their homes.

With lightning speed, before the enemy even knew what hit

them, Abram called the 318 trained men born in his household, and together they went to rescue Lot and his family (Genesis 14:14). God gave Abram the victory, after which the king of Sodom came to meet Abram in the Valley of Shaveh, that is, the King's Valley. The king of Sodom said to Abram, "Give me the people and keep the goods for yourself." But Abram said to the king of Sodom, "I have raised my hand to the Lord God Most High, Creator of heaven and earth, and have taken an oath that I will accept nothing belonging to you, not even a thread or the thong of a sandal so that you will never be able to say, 'I made Abram rich'" (Genesis 14:21-23).

This encounter says much more than the words we read. It certainly sounds like Abram came to realize his blessings were from God and God alone, and that he did not need or even desire anyone else's riches. He learned a lot from his years in Haran and Egypt. Now that he was in the place where God wanted him, he was not going to risk losing it.

Where do you find yourself in your walk with God? Do you depend on yourself, as well as others, for your provision? Do you spend countless hours worrying about what you don't have? Do you work so many hours that you neglect your home and family, and then complain because you never hear from God? Maybe it's time to take a deep breath, count your blessings and begin relying on the Lord God Most High, Creator of heaven and earth, to bring you to the place He wants you to be. Then, like Abram, He can provide all that you need.

Lord, You alone know my needs, wants and desires. May I come to the place where I rely on You to fill them all, giving You and You alone the praise You are worthy to receive. In the name of Jesus, I pray. Amen.

DAY 37

MELCHIZEDEK
Read Genesis 14:17-24

Undertaking a study of the Old Testament at times overwhelms me with a flood of emotions, especially when a passage has significance, yet it's difficult to fully comprehend what that significance is. Such is the case with Melchizedek, King of Salem. After Abram's victory which we read about yesterday, we are introduced to Melchizedek, "the mysterious." I say "mysterious" because he suddenly appears on the scene, then, other than Psalm 110, he is not mentioned again in the Old Testament. Yet in the New Testament we are told he had no mother or father, is without genealogy, without beginning of days or end of life and, like the Son of God, remains a priest forever (Hebrews 7:3).

In his brief encounter with Abram, Melchizedek served him bread and wine. This could have been for the purpose of renewal and refreshment, for surely Abram was exhausted from the battle on his return journey home. It could also represent what took place in the New Testament when Jesus served communion to his disciples at the last Passover meal before his crucifixion.

Melchizedek gave a blessing to Abram, which he said was from God Most High...who delivered Abram's enemies into his hands. After this, Abram gave a tenth of everything he won in the battle to Melchizedek, something we now refer to as the tithe. So, my understanding from listening to hours of sermons, doing research, and spending time in prayer, is that Melchizedek was the forerunner in the Old Testament of who Christ is in the New Testament. His appearance to Abram established the eternal and everlasting Royal Priesthood that now comes through Jesus Christ, who died for our sins once for all, who was raised from the dead and who is now seated at the right hand of God and intercedes for us (Romans 8:34). So while Abram was the father of God's promise in the Old Testament and was blessed by Melchizedek, it is Jesus who is perfect forever and is the fulfillment of that promise in the New Testament. Jesus is a priest forever in the order of Melchizedek (Hebrews 7:11 & Psalm 110:4).

Lord, open my heart and mind to the meaning of Your word this day. Give me the wisdom and revelation I need so that I might know You better—You who are God Almighty and the One who lives forever and ever! Amen.

DAY 38

RIGHTEOUSNESS
Read Genesis 15:1-6

During a somewhat heated conversation with a family member who isn't convinced the Bible is the Word of God, he told me emphatically, "Well, I am righteous." The neurons in my brain began to race in all directions when I heard that statement and I was unable to give a response. I thought of one later, but it was too late. That seems to happen to me more than I like to admit. We ended our conversation agreeing to disagree, and I hung up the phone shaking my head, wondering out loud, "What does he base his righteousness on?" Unfortunately, we never revisited that conversation, at least not yet, but understanding righteousness and how we attain it brings us back to the life of Abram.

We know that although Abram listened to God, he wasn't perfect. He lied to Pharaoh to save his own skin and instead of going directly to the Promised Land, he dawdled along the way. It's probable to assume he learned lessons from these mistakes as he talked with God about what troubled him, such as, having no heir to pass down the promise that his offspring would be like "the dust of the earth" (Genesis 13:16). God reiterated His promise when He took Abram outside his tent and said, "Look up at the heavens and count the stars, if indeed you can count them. So shall your offspring be" (Genesis 15:5).

The words that follow are the beginning of the hope that intricately winds its way through the entirety of the Bible: "Abram believed the Lord, and He credited it to him as righteousness." In other words, because Abram in his heart of hearts believed what God told him, even though so much pointed in another direction, God blotted out all the wrongdoing that took place in Abram's life and credited his belief in Him as righteousness. Righteousness means: right; just; upright, especially free from wrong, guilt or sin; virtuous; worthy. That is some pretty powerful stuff.

There is no other religion on earth that gives that kind of freedom from sin. Furthermore, because the words "it was credited to him" we're written not for him alone, but for those who believe in Him who raised Jesus our Lord from the dead - God will also credit them righteousness (Romans 4:23). Our righteousness comes through belief in the One who not only died for our sins, but was raised to life for our justification. We don't make ourselves righteous, but it is credited to us as righteousness when we believe in Jesus Christ as our Lord and Savior. What a hope and promise! It all began with Abram who at 86 years of age believed what God said.

Lord, search me and know my ways. If there is anything hidden deep within me that prevents me from fully believing in You with all my heart, take it from me so that, as Abram, I may believe what You say without question, so that it will be credited to me as righteousness. In the precious name of Jesus, I pray. Amen.

DAY 39

GOD'S FAITHFULNESS
Read Genesis 15:7-8

Has there ever been a time in your life when you were so sure of God that you felt invincible, that there was nothing that would shake your faith? I have. There was a time when I told someone in no uncertain terms, "Oh, I would NEVER do that!" Wouldn't you know, it wasn't very long after that until the very thing I said I would never do, I did. There's something about our words and our actions that we should not forget: God hears and sees them all (Psalm 94:9).

Being a believer in Jesus Christ does not take away our humanness. We still make mistakes. So it was with Abram, for right after he believed God about an heir, the Lord also said to him, "I am the Lord, who brought you out of Ur of the Chaldeans to give you this land to take possession of it." But Abram said, "O Sovereign Lord, how can I know that I will gain possession of it?" Though Abram was uncertain how God was going to accomplish this promise, the Lord was undeterred. He doesn't change His mind and take away His promise just because we don't understand or we do something wrong. For the word of the Lord is right and true; He is faithful in all He does (Psalm 33:4). The Lord is faithful to all His promises and loving toward all He has made. He upholds all those who fall and lifts up all who are bowed down (Psalm 145: 13-14). This same God tells us in the New Testament that He has reconciled us by Christ's physical body through death to present us holy in His sight, without blemish and free from accusation – if we continue in our faith, established and firm, not moved from the hope held out in the gospel (Colossians 1:22-23). Abram had faith, yet he wasn't sure how God was going to fulfill His promise. We too may have doubts and fears that hold us back from receiving all God has for us, but we can be certain of one thing: He is a God who does not lie (Numbers 23:19).

When He tells us we are reconciled to Him by Christ's physical body through death, we can count on it. When He says we are without blemish and free from accusation if we continue in our faith, we can trust that He will forgive us when we fall. His ways are so much higher than our ways, and His thoughts than our thoughts (Isaiah 55:9). We can trust Him implicitly for He gives us our very breath and when we call out to Him He hears our cry and saves us (Psalm 145:19).

Lord, how can I praise You enough, how can I thank You enough, for all Your promises and for all Your love toward me? Thank You that in my humanness, You have made a way to be reconciled to You not only as I walk this earth, but forever in eternity. Help me to remain faithful by calling upon You in everything I think, do, and say. In the name of Jesus, I pray. Amen.

DAY 40

THE BLOOD COVENANT
Read Genesis 15:9-21

What I love most about the Bible is its honesty, especially when it comes to the humanness of those that are written about. Abram believed God when He told him his descendants would be like the stars in the sky and God credited it to him as righteousness. However, in the very next paragraph when God showed Abram the land his descendants would one day possess, Abram said, "O Sovereign Lord, how will I know that I will gain possession of the land?" (Genesis 15:8).

So God instructed Abram to prepare three animals and cut them in half, along with a dove and pigeon. In those days, a covenant between two people was made by cutting animals in half, then walking between the halves, representing a solemn oath between the two parties that could not be broken. Abram did as the Lord instructed. Then he waited and waited and waited. All day long, nothing happened, except birds of prey came down on the carcasses and Abram drove them away. As the sun was setting, Abram fell into a deep sleep and a thick and dreadful darkness came over him. Then the Lord spoke to Abram saying, "Know for certain that your descendants will be strangers in a country not their own, and they will be enslaved and mistreated 400 years. But I will punish the nation they serve as slaves, and afterward they will come out with great possessions. You, however, will go to your fathers in peace and be buried at a good old age. In the fourth generation, your descendants will come back here, for the sin of the Amorites has not yet reached its full measure" (Genesis 15:9-18).

When Abram awoke, darkness had fallen. It was then that a smoking firepot with a blazing torch appeared and passed between the animal halves. On that day the Lord made a covenant with Abram and said, "To your descendants I give this land, from the river of Egypt to the great river, the Euphrates…" When the fire passed between the pieces, this represented the power of God making a covenant with Abram that what He said would one day be fulfilled.

Today, we live in an instant and on-demand society where we think no matter what we want, it should be given to us immediately, but that is not God's way. He tells us many times throughout Scripture to be patient, and this is what He was saying to Abram. "I am telling you all this but it will not happen in your lifetime. Right now there is a group of people in the land (the Amorites) whose behavior has not reached the level of wickedness that the land should be taken from them, but that time will come. Before it does, your descendants will be slaves in a foreign land for 400 years. It will be a dark and dismal time. They will feel forsaken by Me, but I will hear their cry and deliver them. Then they will inherit the land. This is My solemn oath to you, Abram."

God also made a covenant with us by sending Jesus to die for our sins; but we must patiently wait for the fulfillment of all that

He told us will one day come to pass. Jesus will return to this earth, and of His kingdom, there will be no end (Isaiah 9:7).

Lord, may I have patience as I await the coming of the Savior Jesus Christ. Amen.

DAY 41

HEIRS
Read Genesis 16:1-4

How do you make sense of a sordid love triangle, especially when one of those involved is a righteous man of God? One way is to possibly justify it by tradition, like that which may have been common in Ur of the Chaldeans, where Abram and Sarai were originally from. It was an accepted practice that men could have children by their slave women if their wife was unable to bear children. So, when Sarai suggested to Abram that he sleep with her maidservant so she could bear a son, Abram agreed. After all, it had been 10 years since God promised an heir. Wasn't that long enough to wait?

There is no mention that Abram prayed to the Lord before making this decision, but he didn't have to. He already knew the answer. God told him his offspring would be more than the stars in the sky (Genesis 15:5), and he knew that Sarai was his wife; not Hagar.

There are times I read this story and say, "What was he

thinking? God spoke to him directly. Couldn't he have been patient and waited?" However, I feel a prick in my heart at my own impatience. By that I mean I know how it all began, and I know how it ends because God told me in His Word. It is the time between the beginning and end that makes it so difficult to be patient.

Jesus told John the Apostle in Revelation 22:12, "Behold, I am coming soon! My reward is with me and I will give to everyone according to what he has done." Though we do not know the day or hour of His return (not even Jesus does), we can be certain it will happen. Having said that, over the 40-plus years of my Christian walk, if I'm completely honest, I have often been impatient, sometimes wondering why it has taken so long and Jesus has not yet returned.

When Paul wrote to the Galatians, he was also writing to us. "Let us not become weary in doing good, for at the proper time we will reap a harvest if we do not give up" (Galatians 6:9). Despite Abram's act of adultery, God did not withdraw His promise, for Abram believed and God credited it to him as righteousness.

Though there may be times we sin, He is faithful and just to forgive us our sins (1 John 1:9) and He will not withdraw from us His promise of eternity with Him. As Jesus said on the cross, "It is finished," which means His purpose for coming was complete, and that will never change. Just like God promised Abram an heir, He promises us we too are His heirs (Galatians 3:29), if we believe and trust in Him.

Lord, give me the strength and faith to remain faithful to You until the end. In the precious name of Jesus, I pray. Amen.

DAY 42

TAKING RESPONSIBILITY
Read Genesis 16:5-8

Had Abram waited patiently and told Sarai, "God has a different plan," there would have been no adultery and no Ishmael. Still, like the brilliance of a noonday sun, the light of God's word never sugarcoats the people who are written about. We see them as they are and, like us, they have their faults. So Abram slept with Hagar and she conceived. Something happened, though, which Sarai was unprepared for: Hagar despised Sarai. Then Sarai said to Abram, "You are responsible for the wrong I am suffering" (Genesis 16:5). Wow, I bet he didn't see that coming. He could have said, "It was your idea. Live with it." Instead, he told Sarai, "Do with her whatever you want" (Genesis 16:6).

Sarai gave her husband an earthly solution to a problem she perceived was causing him grave concern. He took her advice, but when trouble began. He didn't want to deal with it and told Sarai it was her responsibility to take care of it. Sounds like a familiar refrain when we look back to Adam. He not only refused to take responsibility for his actions, but he also blamed God for "the woman that you put here with me" (Genesis 3:12).

It is wrong when we refuse to take responsibility for our own actions. It often causes great suffering for others, as Hagar would soon discover. Sarai treated Hagar so badly that Hagar ran away. Still, running away from our problems never solves them, it only compounds them. The more compounded they become, the more our hearts potentially harden toward God (Proverbs 28:13-14). The Lord was not going to allow Abram to pretend he had no responsibility in a situation that was of his own doing. As we will read tomorrow, God did not abandon Hagar but sent her back to Sarai and Abram where she and her child would be cared for.

Paul wrote in Colossians 3:25, "Anyone who does wrong will be repaid for the wrong he does, and there is no favoritism." However, if we confess our sins, God is faithful and just to forgive us our sins and purify us from all unrighteousness (1 John 1:9). Our Lord is a faithful and loving God who wants nothing more than a repentant heart and pure honesty when it comes to taking responsibility for our actions and our sins. And why not? He already knows everything there is to know about us.

Lord, forgive me for ever trying to hide anything from You. Cleanse me and make me whole through the precious blood of Jesus, the One who died for my sins. Amen.

DAY 43

THE RETURN
Read Genesis 16:9-16

What must Hagar have been thinking as she fled for her life toward Egypt? "How did I get into this mess? It wasn't my idea to sleep with Abram." Here she was alone, frightened and carrying a married man's child. What was she to do? Running to the point of exhaustion, she found refreshment at the spring called Beer Lahai Roi, which means, "well of the Living One who sees me." This is where the angel of the Lord found her, and he said, "Hagar, servant of Sarai, where have you come from and where are you going?" (Genesis 16:8).

The angel did not address Hagar as Abram's wife, but as Sarai's servant, which was an indication of what her true position was in the family. Hagar, most likely startled, hot and dirty, with tears running down her cheeks, answered, "I am running away from my mistress Sarai." With a voice that brought comfort like cool, soothing lotion on dry, cracked skin, the angel said, "Go back to your mistress and submit to her...You are now with child and you will have a son. You shall name him Ishmael, meaning God has heard, for the Lord has heard of your misery" (Genesis 16:9-11).

Sarai's plan went awry, but God saw Hagar in her place of need and promised that if she returned she and her son would be cared for. So Hagar returned and submitted herself to her mistress Sarai. She bore a son, and Abram named him Ishmael. The angel told Hagar Ishmael "would be a wild donkey of a man; his hand will be against everyone and everyone's hand against him, and he will live in hostility toward all his brothers." That does not sound like the son of promise about whom God had spoken to Abram, and he wasn't, but more about that later.

What we can learn is that despite our own failings, God loves us. We may have made many choices ending in bad results - some of our own doing, some because of what others have done, but God can use our life experiences for His purposes when we humble ourselves before Him and do as He directs us to do. Hagar did. She humbled herself before the God who saw her and submitted to Sarai for many years as she raised her son. He would become the father of 12 tribes, and from those tribes would come some of the Arabs as we know today. Just as the angel told Hagar, "...he will live in hostility toward all his brothers," we can see those results now taking place.

The Lord not only saw Hagar, but He also sees each and every one of us. He knows we make mistakes, but He tells us in His word that He gives grace to the humble and that if we humble ourselves before Him, He will lift us up (James 4:6 & 10).

Lord, thank you for your plan of salvation through Your Son Jesus Christ, the One who became as one of us, who humbled Himself to the point of death on a cross so that we can be set free from our sins. Humble me in Your presence and make me more like Jesus every day of my life. In His precious name, I pray, Amen.

DAY 44

LAUGHTER
Read Genesis 17-18:15

Thirteen years passed and Abram was now 99 years old, Sarai 89. We can imagine that Abram loved his son Ishmael while Sarai regretted it every day of her life. This is conjecture, but one thing is certain, God was not yet finished with Abram and Sarai. It was a new day and God had something very specific in mind, which so humbled Abram he fell facedown before the Lord. And God said to him, "As for Me, this is my covenant with you: You will be the father of many nations. No longer will you be called Abram. Your name will be Abraham, for I have made you a father of many nations..." He told Abraham, "I will establish my covenant as an everlasting covenant...to be your God and the God of your descendants after you" (Genesis 17:3-7). Similar to marriage, it was a solemn oath, a promise never meant to be broken. Just like a ring is the symbol of an unending commitment, circumcision of all males eight days and older became the symbol of this covenant between Abraham and God.

God also said to Abraham, "As for Sarai your wife, you are no longer to call her Sarai. Her name will be Sarah. I will bless her and will surely give you a son by her." At this news, Abraham fell facedown again but this time he laughed to himself, perhaps thinking God would not hear as he whispered, "Will a son be born to a man 100 years old? Will Sarah bear a child at the age of 90?" Then he said to God, "If only Ishmael might live under your blessing" (Genesis 17:17-18).

God told Abraham that Ishmael would be blessed because of him, but he was not the heir. God announced His everlasting covenant was to be with Isaac (meaning laughter), the son whom Sarah would have one year later. Soon thereafter, three visitors came and confirmed to Abraham that he and Sarah would have a son and name him Isaac. Sarah, who was listening to the conversation, also laughed. At her age, no way! But the Lord heard her laugh and said, "Is there anything too hard for the Lord?" Sarah denied that she laughed, but the Lord said to her, "Yes, you did laugh." God hears us, and when He speaks such things, it is not in jest (Matthew 12:36-37).

Lord, Your word is so precise in every detail. You knew from the time Adam and Eve sinned that You would choose Abraham to be the father of all nations and the one from whose lineage the Messiah would come. Thank you for Your plan of salvation that is available to everyone who believes. In the name of Jesus, I pray. Amen.

DAY 45

INTERCESSION
Read Genesis 18:16-33

When the three visitors came to visit Abraham and Sarah, it was a turning point in their relationship with Him. Both of them were given new names, they were told they would have a son within one year and an everlasting covenant was made between Abraham and God. As the visitors were leaving, something extraordinary occurred. Abraham walked alongside to see them on their way, and the Lord asked Himself a question, "Shall I hide from Abraham what I am about to do? Abraham will surely become a great and powerful nation, and all nations on earth will be blessed through him" (Genesis 18:17-18).

Apparently Abraham did not know where the three were going or what was about to take place as they departed. What I find extraordinary about this passage is that God was debating whether He should reveal to Abraham what was about to happen, then went on to conclude, "Why, yes, of course, I should." Otherwise, Abraham might have thought the destruction of Sodom and the surrounding cities were a natural disaster, and not an intentional act of destruction due to their wickedness. Then the Lord said to Abraham, "The outcry against Sodom and Gomorrah is so great and their sin so grievous that I will go down and see if what they have done is as bad as the outcry that has reached Me. If not, I will know" (Genesis 18:21).

The other two visitors turned away and went toward Sodom, but Abraham remained standing before the Lord. As they stood face to face, Abraham interceded for Sodom and Gomorrah, "What if there are 50 righteous people in the city? Will you really sweep it away and not spare the place for the sake of the 50 righteous people in it...Will not the Judge of all the earth do right?" The Lord responded that He would spare the cities for the sake of 50, which emboldened Abraham to keep asking by decreasing the number, ending with, "May the Lord not be angry but let me speak just once more. What if only 10 can be found there?" The Lord answered, "For the sake of 10, I will not destroy it" (Genesis 18:26-32).

This interchange tells us that our Lord is not only just, but He is merciful. As wicked as He would find Sodom and Gomorrah, He was willing to spare everyone for 10 righteous people. As Abraham interceded in this situation, we too have someone who intercedes for us. His name is Christ Jesus, who died – more than that, who was raised to life – and is at the right hand of God and is also interceding for us (Romans 8:34).

Lord, You who are just yet merciful, thank You for sending Your Son Jesus, who is now sitting at Your right hand and interceding for us. It is in His precious name that we praise You. Amen.

DAY 46

THE LORD, RICH IN LOVE
Read Genesis 19:1-11

Sodom and Gomorrah, the infamous cities of the plain that most people have heard of, but may not know why, are located by the Dead Sea at the lowest known place on earth. They were the furthest away from heaven as one could get. It was the place where Lot ended up living when he parted ways with his "Uncle Abraham." The two angels arrived at Sodom in the evening, and Lot was sitting in the gateway of the city. Isn't it interesting that when they visited Abraham, it was during the heat of the day, in bright sunlight, where everything was exposed and open? Then, by the time they arrived in Sodom, it was evening, the time when it is dark and things are hidden.

When Lot saw them coming, he got up and urged them to come stay with him, then leave early in the morning. They answered, "No, we will spend the night in the square." That would be equivalent to one of us going into an area known for its high crime rate to stay the night. Lot wasn't about to let that happen. He insisted strongly, that they come with him, stay at his house, and eat (Genesis 19:3).

Before they went to bed, all the men from every part of the city of Sodom, both young and old, surrounded Lot's house. They called out, "Where are the men who came to you tonight? Bring them out to us so that we can have sex with them." Lot was horrified, but the evil in that place had dulled his senses and he offered his two virgin daughters to these men to do with them what they pleased. That wasn't what the men wanted, so they began to put pressure on Lot and moved forward to break down the door to his house. It was then that the angels inside the house reached for Lot and pulled him back into the house, shutting the door. Then they struck the men outside the house with blindness so that they could not find the door.

What a terrifying experience this must have been for everyone. It was apparent to the angels that there were not even 10 righteous people. So they told Lot the cities were about to be destroyed and to gather everyone who belonged to him and get them out immediately. The outcries against the city were true. There was such wickedness in the land that it could no longer be tolerated by God. It was judgment time, though Lot and his family would be spared if they believed and got out with their lives.

There are times in today's world it feels like Sodom and Gomorrah when watching the news or listening to radio, and I wonder why God doesn't just end it all. Then I read 2 Peter 3:9, which tells us, "The Lord is not slow in keeping His promise, as some understand slowness. He is patient... not wanting anyone to perish but everyone to come to repentance."

So, like Sodom, His judgment is certain to one day come, but in the words of King David we are told to "wait for the Lord; be strong and take heart and wait for the Lord" (Psalm 27:14). The Lord is gracious and compassionate. He is slow to anger and rich in love. The Lord is good to all; He has compassion on all He has made (Psalm 145:8-9).

Thank You, Lord, for Your compassion and rich love toward all You have made. Help me reflect who You are so that others will see You in me and desire the same. In the name of Jesus, I pray. Amen.

DAY 47

NO JOKE
Read Genesis 19:12-20

Imagine Lot running frantically throughout the streets of Sodom desperate to save his family from the coming destruction. "Son, get ready to leave immediately. The angels who came to see me last night said the city and everyone in it are going to be destroyed. You must leave." Then imagine his despair when his sons-in-law looked at him in disbelief as though he were a mad man, laughing in his face as though it were a practical joke, then shutting the door in his face (Genesis 19:14). We live today as though this could never happen, yet in a moment's time our entire country went on lockdown because of an unseen enemy that lurked in unknown places with the potential to kill thousands upon thousands, and millions lost their jobs.

If we have read our Bibles, we know of another event that will certainly take place known as the end times, but even now when preachers and Christians tell the world about coming judgment, most people shake their heads in disbelief and say it is a joke or just downright craziness.

Consider what Jesus said in Matthew 24:38 about the end days, "For in the days before the flood, people were eating and drinking, marrying and giving in marriage, up to the day Noah entered the ark and they knew nothing about what would happen until the flood came and took them all away...Therefore keep watch, because you do not know on what day your Lord will come." That day will come, and once it does, there is no turning back as Lot's wife did when they fled Sodom. There will be nothing to go back to (2 Peter 2:4-10).

Paul writes to the Philippians: "But one thing I do: Forgetting what is behind and straining toward what is ahead. I press on toward the goal to win the prize for which God has called me heavenward in Christ Jesus" (3:13). The goal is eternal life for which all of us should strive (Colossians 3:2).

Lord, the day I asked Jesus to forgive me of my sins and come into my life, I have not looked back. I know what I left behind and I don't want to go back. Help each and every one of us take hold of that which You promise and be prepared for the day when Jesus will appear in all His glory to set up His kingdom of which there will be no end. Amen.

DAY 48

FAITH VERSUS FEAR
Read Genesis 19:27-38

The smoke from the valley filled the air where fire and brimstone fell onto Sodom and Gomorrah and the cities of the plains. Abraham stood high atop the mountain looking down, not knowing if Lot and his family escaped. Lot did escape, though barely, and he went to Zoar, where sadly the story about him does not end well. With his wife gone, he is left with his two daughters. We are not told how Lot was coping, but it seems he may have lost faith in God. As he began to fear those around him, he and his daughters left Zoar to live in a cave.

Though caves are known to have a consistent temperature, they are dark, damp, and not the least bit inviting when it comes to everyday living. Not to excuse their behavior, but Lot's daughters must have given up all hope that they would marry and have children. Having grown up in Sodom, who is to say what perversions they were exposed to. They came up with a plan under the guise of preserving their father's lineage. They must have had some semblance of conscience, though, as they knew their father wouldn't approve, so they got him drunk before carrying out their ill-conceived plan. After they got him drunk, the oldest daughter was the first to have sex with their father, and then the following night there was a repeat with the youngest. Both became pregnant, and for generations to come the descendants of these two incestuous boys would be a thorn in the side of God's chosen people. The oldest daughter's son became the father of what were known as the Moabites and the younger daughter's son was the father of the Ammonites.

Though we may never come up with the sort of plan that Lot's daughters did, we say and do things, perhaps only once, that can change the trajectory of our lives. These things can divert us far from the plans God has or had for us. There is a way to avoid such a collision of our faith and our fears, and that is by reading God's word and constantly being in an attitude of prayer (Philippians 4:6). When we allow each day to fade away without giving an iota of attention to our faith, it begins to drift away like smoke from a chimney, ultimately leaving behind a pile of ashes.

You might ask: How do I make time for God when the pressures of life are vying for my attention? The more thought-provoking question might be: How can I cope with the pressures of life without making time for God? When Jesus said, "Seek first the Kingdom of God and his righteousness and all these things (what to eat, drink or wear) will be added to you" (Matthew 6:33), He wasn't making a suggestion. He was giving a command, and for good reason. It works. I've heard numerous accounts of God's people being at the brink of disaster, nowhere to turn, not knowing where they would sleep or if they would eat. Nevertheless, because they trusted their Redeemer, He made a way and provided for their needs.

I'm not saying we should sit on our backsides all day, saying prayers and waiting for things to happen. It doesn't work that way. We must trust God to guide us by His Spirit, but we need to also do our part. Had Lot done that, he may not have left Zoar, and the events we just read about would most likely have not taken place.

Lord, help me not to be judge and jury when it comes to Lot and his daughters but give me the ability to learn from their mistakes. May I be quick to confess my own sins and ask Your forgiveness and mercy. In the name of Jesus, I pray. Amen.

DAY 49

INWARD BEAUTY
Read Genesis 20:1-2

*L*ately, when I look in the mirror, one, two, sometimes even three new wrinkles seem to magically appear on my face and/or neck, and I wonder, "How can this be happening? It was only yesterday I was a teenager." Then my mind wanders to those botox and old-age cream commercials on TV. I find myself getting sucked into the imaginary world of looking younger, no matter my age, quickly waking up to the reality that the models in those ads are maybe 30 years old, if you stretch it. There's no way any of those products are going to make a 60-something year old look 30 again. Ain't happening!

So what's my point? Well, when Abraham and Sarah moved on from the place where Abraham had stood before the Lord into the region of the Negev (toward Egypt), they stopped for a while at a place called Gerar, where they met Abimelech, its king. Convinced that there was no fear of God there, and that the king would kill him and take his wife, Abraham lied to this king and instructed Sarah to do likewise. Sound familiar? Except this is 25 years after telling the same lie to Pharaoh, king of Egypt. You would think Abraham would have learned his lesson, but it seems he lost sight of God and decided to take matters into his own hands again. How easily we revert back to our human ways when we allow our fear to overcome our faith.

Because of this lie, Abimelech took Sarah into his harem. Well into her 80s at this point, Sarah is getting pretty old, which makes it all the more amazing that this king would find her attractive. Still, Sarah's beauty and grace did not come from her outward appearance. As Proverbs 30:31 tells us, "Charm is deceptive and beauty is fleeting, but a woman who fears the Lord is to be praised." And in the New Testament, Peter put it so well when he wrote to God's elect, "your beauty should not come from outward adornment... Instead, it should be that of your inner self, the unfading beauty of a gentle and quiet spirit, which is of great worth in God's sight. For this is the way holy women of the past, who put their hope in God, used to make themselves beautiful. They were submissive to their own husbands, like Sarah, who obeyed Abraham and called him her master" (1 Peter 3:1-7).

The next time I stand in front of a mirror and count my wrinkles, I will think back to Sarah as a reminder that no matter my age, real beauty comes from within, the beauty which reflects the inner peace, humility and love only our Savior can give - an everlasting beauty that does not fade away with age.

Lord, thank You for Your gentle reminder that youth quickly fades and life is but a moment in time. As Paul writes to the Colossians, may we clothe ourselves with compassion, kindness, humility, gentleness and patience—all the virtues that come from within. In the name of Jesus, I pray. Amen.

DAY 50

ABIMELECH, ABRAHAM AND SARAH
Read Genesis 20:3-18

Abimelech realized he had been blind-sided by Abraham and Sarah when God visited him in a dream saying, "You are as good as dead because of the woman you have taken; she is a married woman." Claiming innocence, Abimelech responded, "Lord, will you destroy an innocent nation? Did Abraham not say to me that 'She is my sister,' and did Sarah not say, 'He is my brother'? I have done this with a clear conscience and clean hands." God's answer was, "Yes, I know you did this with a clear conscience...That is why I did not let you touch her. Now return the man's wife, for he is a prophet, and he will pray for you and you will live" (Genesis 20:3-7).

Here we have a pagan king who, in this instance, is more righteous than God's prophet Abraham. However, God instructs Abimelech to not only return Sarah to her husband but to ask Abraham to pray for him so that he will live. Abraham must have been pretty embarrassed when Abimelech asked for his prayers.

God does have a way of humbling us. Do you get the impression that even though God is not pleased with Abraham's behavior, Abraham has not lost favor with the Lord? After all, they were in covenant, something which is not to be broken.

Now Abimelech did that which God instructed him to do, but not without giving Abraham a piece of his mind saying, "What have you done to us? How have I wronged you that you have brought such great guilt upon me and my kingdom? You have done things to me that should not be done. What was your reason for doing this?" (Genesis 20:9). Abraham replied, "I said to myself, 'There is surely no fear of God in this place, and they will kill me because of my wife.'" He went on to explain how he and Sarah agreed on their plan of deception.

After his confession, Abimelech brought sheep and cattle, as well as slaves, and gave them to Abraham. In returning Sarah to him, Abimelech said, "My land is before you; live where you like." Then Abimelech absolved Sarah of any wrongdoing, for he knew she lied to him in obedience to her husband. He said to her, "I am giving your brother (Abraham) a thousand shekels of silver. This is to cover the offense against you before all who are with you; you are completely vindicated." Then Abraham prayed to God, and God healed Abimelech, his wife and his slave girls so they could have children again, for the Lord had closed up every womb in Abimelech's household because of Abraham's wife Sarah.

Before this incident, God spoke to Abraham and Sarah that within the year they would have an heir, the son of promise. Although they knew this, they fell for a trap which we can surmise was Satan's plan to thwart God's plan. As long as she was in Abimelech's harem, Abraham and Sarah were separated. How then was this son to be born? Ultimately, God had spoken, and it was His authority that prevailed.

We can be certain from the events that took place in this story that God does not forsake His children when they fail Him. Once someone becomes a follower of Jesus Christ, a covenant is entered into, and other than the sin of blasphemy of the Holy Spirit (Mark 3:29), there is nothing else in Scripture that tells us He will permanently leave us. It took a pagan king to remind Abraham of that. Let's pray that our dedication to Jesus is so cemented in His word that we won't need an unbeliever to remind us of our commitment to serve our Lord and King.

Heavenly Father, thank You for Your not-so-subtle reminder of what can happen when I take my eyes off of You. Help me to keep my commitment to You daily by reading Your word and being in prayer. Help me also to remember that my struggle is not against flesh and blood but against an enemy who is always looking for ways to embarrass and shame me. May I clothe myself with the armor of Your protection which You have so generously given me to put on. In the holy name of Jesus, I pray. Amen.

DAY 51

GOD IS NEVER IN A HURRY
Read Genesis 21:1-7

Twenty-five years after God told Abraham his descendants would be like the stars in the sky, too innumerable to count, Isaac, the son of promise, was born. It's pretty obvious that God is never in a hurry. In contrast to us, who are always in a hurry.

"Now the Lord was gracious to Sarah as He had said, and the Lord did for Sarah what He had promised. Sarah became pregnant and bore a son to Abraham in his old age, at the very time God had promised him" (Genesis 21:2).

In these two sentences, we learn that God is gracious and that He keeps His promises. Are those not the virtues we look for in others but rarely find? How glorious that we can be in relationship with the God of the universe who is gracious and keeps His promises. He told Abraham and Sarah they would have a son and when he would arrive.

We will learn some time later from other Old Testament

Scripture that God foretold of another son, His very own, that would be born. He also said that this Son (Jesus) will come again, this time to rule with power and authority, and of His kingdom there will be no end (Isaiah 9:7). We can know with certainty that this too will come to pass. Up to now, God has a one hundred percent track record of keeping His word.

Sarah's laughter, which once came because of unbelief, was now laughter of sheer joy as she held her precious son in her arms, giving thanks to God for keeping His promise in their old age. There have been numerous times, and even to this day, when my prayers seem to go unanswered and I grow impatient. However, when I sit in the solitude of His presence and read what is written in His word, knowing that His promises are true, I become more willing to wait patiently for His answers. God's timing is always perfect. We can count on it.

Thank You, Lord, for yet another lesson on how gracious, loving and kind You are toward me. Help me when my impatience interferes with what You know is best. Fill me with the wonder and awe of Your Spirit, knowing that You hear my prayers and You will answer in Your perfect timing. In the name of Jesus, I pray. Amen.

DAY 52

BORN OF THE FLESH OR OF THE SPIRIT?
Read Genesis 21:8-21

There was a big problem brewing which came to a head when Isaac was weaned and Abraham held a great feast in celebration. It was then that Sarah witnessed Ishmael mocking his little brother in such a way as to alarm her, and she feared for Isaac's safety. She immediately went to Abraham and insisted that he not only send Ishmael away, but also Hagar. Abraham was distressed by this, but God spoke to him and said, "Do not be so distressed about the boy and your maidservant. Listen to whatever Sarah tells you because it is through Isaac that your offspring will be reckoned" (Genesis 21:10-12). Isaac, a forerunner of Christ in ways that we will soon learn about, was God's chosen one. The time came for Isaac to take his rightful place in Abraham's family.

Early the next morning Abraham took some food and a skin of water, and gave them to Hagar. He set them on her shoulders, then sent her off with the boy... where they wandered in the desert of Beersheba. It was a difficult journey for them through the desert. Hagar thought they were both going to die, but God spoke to her and said, "Lift the boy up and take him by the hand, for I will make him into a great nation." Then God opened Hagar's eyes and she saw a well of water from which she and her son drank. God was with the boy as he grew up (Genesis 21:14-20).

Ishmael and Isaac represent a deep divide in the human race. What is this divide between these two sons? I have tried expressing my thoughts on this subject, but I came up short. The words of my favorite preacher, David Pawson, explain it best, "It is the division between Israeli and Arab. That is a bad enough division, but that is not the deepest gulf in the human race. It is the division between Jew and Gentile. That, too, is not the deepest division between the human race. It is basically the division between those who are born of the flesh and those who are born of the spirit. There is no deeper division than that. It cuts the human race right into two and everybody is either an Ishmael, born of the flesh, or an Isaac, born of the spirit."[1]

We are all born an Ishmael. It isn't until we ask Jesus Christ to come into our lives that we become an Isaac. That is our choice. Will we remain in the flesh to which we were born and die in our sins, or will we be born of the spirit and live for Christ? We can live for ourselves (Ishmael/the flesh), doing all the things we think necessary to obtain favor with God, doing good and being kind, thereby trying to make our own way to heaven (which is impossible). Or, we can live for God (Isaac/the spirit) and, as Paul says, die to ourselves every day (1 Corinthians 15:31). Do we want to be sons and daughters born by the slave woman in the ordinary way and remain there? Or, do we want to be sons and daughters born by the free woman who are born as the result of promise (Galatians 4:21-31)? As followers of Jesus Christ, our answer should be evident.

Lord, help me to understand fully the differences between flesh and spirit, slavery and freedom, and help me to always make the choice that honors You and sets me free to be all You want me to be. In the name of Jesus, I pray. Amen.

DAY 53

SEEKING FAVOR
Read Genesis 21:22-34

There is a reason for everything written in the Bible and I'm trying my best to interpret the meaning of most of it by prayer, research and study. Still, in all honesty, I am not quite sure of the significance of the passage in Genesis 21:22-34. From the previous passages, we know that Ishmael and Hagar are now out of the picture and it seems there was a time of peace and quiet for Abraham and his family.

Abimelech and his commander came to Abraham saying, "God is with you in everything you do. Now swear to me here before God that you will not deal falsely with me, my children or my descendants. Show to me and to the country where you are living as an alien the same kindness I have shown you" (Genesis 21:22-23). I'm surmising that because of their previous encounter, Abimelech knew Abraham was a man of God and because of this he wanted to align himself with Abraham and receive not only a blessing, but protection in the event somewhere down the road they needed help. Apparently Abraham knew what Abimelech was asking for because he agreed and said, "I swear it."

Before Abraham agreed to a treaty, there was the slight issue of a well that had been taken from Abraham by some of Abimelech's servants, and he wanted that rectified. Abimelech said, "I don't know who has done this. You did not tell me until I heard it only today." Apparently it was taken care of immediately, and the two men made a treaty. Abraham set apart seven ewe lambs from his flock and Abimelech asked him, "What is the meaning of these seven ewe lambs you have set apart by themselves?"

Abraham replied, "Accept these seven lambs from my hand as a witness that I dug this well," and Abimelech did. That place was called Beersheba, meaning the well of the oath, because the two men swore an oath there.[1]

Then Abimelech and the commander returned to the land of the Philistines. Abraham planted a tamarisk tree in Beersheba, and there he called upon the name of the Lord, the Eternal God. Abraham stayed in the land of the Philistines. This must have been a place of solace where Abraham could commune with God and God with him, something which he most certainly needed for what was about to happen next in his life.

Lord, I don't always understand the meaning of certain passages in Your word, but I know they are there for a reason. I trust that throughout this study You are guiding my thoughts and my writing as I seek You and endeavor to delve into the lives of those who were the building blocks of our identity and faith today. If there is something that someone can gain from today's reading, Lord, may it be so. In the name of Jesus, I pray. Amen.

DAY 54

THE BURNT OFFERING
Read Genesis 22:1-12

There came a time that God tested Abraham by saying, "Take your son, your only son, Isaac, whom you love... Sacrifice him there as a burnt offering..." (Genesis 22:1-2). Imagine God asking any of us to do this. What would our response be? Mine might be, "Have you lost your mind, Lord?" Not Abraham's. He got up early the next morning and saddled his donkey, taking two servants and his son Isaac, as well as the wood for the burnt offering (Genesis 22:3).

God was not asking Abraham to do something He would not do. Though it would be thousands of years later, He too offered His only Son so that whosoever believes in Him will not perish but have eternal life (John 3:16). It's interesting that "on the third day," Abraham saw the place God told him to go, for Jesus was raised from the dead on the third day (Genesis 22:4; Acts 10:40). When Abraham looked up and saw the place (of sacrifice) in the distance, he instructed his servants to stay with the donkey, and only he and Isaac would go to worship and then come back. Jesus went to the Garden of Gethsemane to be alone with His Father (Luke 22:39-44). On their way, Isaac asked his father about the sacrifice. Abraham responded, "God Himself will provide the lamb." Jesus is the Lamb of God who takes away the sins of the world (John 1:29). When they reached the place, Abraham built the altar, then bound his son and laid him on it. He then took the knife to slay him and reached up, yet Isaac never said a word. When taken before Pilate and accused, Jesus still made no reply, and Pilate was amazed (Mark 15:5).

Then the angel of the Lord called out, "Abraham, Abraham, do not lay a hand on the boy...now I know that you fear God because you have not withheld from Me your son, your only son." Abraham looked over to see a ram caught in a bush of thorns to be used as a sacrifice (Genesis 22:11-13). Before Jesus, the Son of God, was crucified, the soldiers placed a crown of thorns on His head and mocked Him saying, "Hail, king of the Jews!" (Mark 15:17-18).

Abraham's faithfulness to God saved his son. God's faithfulness through sacrificing His only Son saves us from our sins (and an eternity in hell without Him). What an amazing story of Abraham's love for God and of God's love for us. Let this penetrate deep into our souls so that we can grasp how wide and long and high and deep is the love of Christ, and to know this love that surpasses knowledge so that we may be filled to the measure of faithfulness of God (Ephesians 3:18).

Lord Jesus, thank You for Your faithfulness in dying on a cross and shedding Your blood for my sins. It is beyond understanding to think You love me this much. Fill me each day with the power of Your Spirit, giving me a greater understanding of this surpassing love that belongs to all who call upon Your precious name. Amen.

DAY 55

GOD'S REWARD FOR FAITHFULNESS
Read Genesis 22:13-24

When Abraham looked up, he saw a ram caught in a thicket by its horns. He took the ram and sacrificed it as a burnt offering instead of his son (Genesis 22:13). What a testimony to Abraham's faithfulness to God. Without question, he followed God's command to offer his son. He was not only rewarded for that faithfulness, his son was restored to him. This alone is enough material for not only a sermon, but an entire study on faithfulness. Anyhow, we will continue.

The angel of the Lord called to Abraham from heaven a second time and said, "I swear by myself...that because you have done this and have not withheld your son, your only son, I will surely bless you and make your descendants as numerous as the stars in the sky and as the sand on the seashore. Your descendants will take possession of the cities of their enemies, and through your offspring all nations on earth will be blessed, because you have obeyed Me" (Genesis 22:16-18). These words, "because you have obeyed Me," remind us of the importance of obedience in order to receive God's blessing. We know that this blessing on Abraham did not come easily.

There is no mention of the emotional turmoil Abraham might have experienced through all of this. However, we know he was a human being, so it's not beyond our imagination to think he struggled. The glorious thing is, he endured the test without complaint and his reward was immeasurable.

May we too be faithful, without complaint, when we walk through the dark times, trusting that God will bring us through and our reward will be great. It may not happen until eternity, but we can rest assured it will indeed happen.

Continuing to the end of chapter twenty-two, verses 20-24 may seem somewhat out of place. By this juncture, we should know that everything written in God's word has a purpose. It's important to know who people are, which may be the reason we are now introduced to Nahor, who was Abraham's brother. He not only had a wife, but he also had a concubine. They both bore him children. Milcah was Nahor's wife. They had eight sons, one of which was Bethuel, the father of Rebekah, who we will soon learn became Isaac's wife.

Lord, I pray that no matter the heartache, no matter the struggle, I will remain faithful to You, without complaint and without worry. Help me to trust that through the darkness You are my light that always shines and points the way. I ask for Your great endurance and patience so that I may joyfully give thanks to You, the One who has qualified me to share in the inheritance of the saints in the kingdom of light (Colossians 1:11-12). In the precious name of Jesus, I pray. Amen.

DAY 56

THE DEATH OF SARAH
Read Genesis 23

If anyone could run out of patience with God, it would have been Abraham. God told him he would inherit the land he was now a stranger and sojourner in, but he had not one piece of property to his name. God also told him that his descendants would not be able to be counted, yet his son was almost 40 years old, unmarried and without children. Then Sarah, who, as we know, had her faults (don't we all?), but she was with Abraham throughout his entire journey and was a caring wife and mother, died at the age of one hundred and twenty-seven. It was a great loss to Abraham, who mourned and wept over her. Nevertheless, he did not mourn and weep endlessly, for he had faith that she was with God.

Death is not something we should ever fear, for this is not our permanent dwelling place where we have an enduring city, but we are looking for the city that is to come (Hebrews 13:14).

In speaking to the disciples, Jesus said, "I tell you the truth, whoever hears my word and believes Him who sent me has eternal life and will not be condemned; he has crossed over from death to life" (John 5:24). Though it is proper and even expected to mourn and weep when we lose loved ones, we should not stay there for long. When our loved ones are gone, in the words of Matthew Henry, we should say, "We are going."[1]

Because Abraham owned no land, he needed to find a burial place for Sarah. In doing so, something happened which he may never have expected. He rose from beside his dead wife and spoke to the Hittites and said, "I am an alien and a stranger among you. Sell me some property for a burial site so I can bury my dead." The Hittites, who were among those who owned and occupied the land, knew Abraham was a sojourner and they weren't so certain they wanted to sell him any land, so they hemmed and hawed, offering to give him their fields to use so he could bury her on their land. Abraham insisted, and as was, and still is, a Middle Eastern custom, Ephron, the Hittite, said, "... the land is worth 400 shekels of silver. But what is that between you and me? Bury your dead" (Genesis 23:15). In other words, if you want to pay this price, you can have the land. So they agreed. The land was deeded to Abraham as his property in the presence of all the Hittites who had come to the gate of the city" (Genesis 23:16-18). It took the death of Abraham's wife to see the beginning of God's promise to him. He finally owned a small piece of the Promised Land.

Lord, thank You for Abraham's life and the example of true faith that he gave so many years ago. In difficult times of loss, help me never to forget that this earth is, indeed, not my permanent home, but that You have prepared a place for me that I have not even imagined. May the eyes of my heart be enlightened in order that I may know the hope to which You have called me, the riches of Your glorious inheritance in the saints and Your incomparably great power for those who believe (Ephesians 1:18). In the name of Jesus, I pray. Amen.

DAY 57

A SOLEMN OATH
Read Genesis 24:1-9

With the death of Sarah, Abraham's focus turned to finding a wife for his son Isaac, who was single and almost 40 years old. We might think it strange that a 40 year old man was allowing his father to choose a wife for him, but it was a custom of the time. Abraham didn't want just any wife for his son. He wanted someone who had the same values and beliefs in God as they did. This did not include the women of Canaan, the land where they were living, which God had promised would one day belong to Abraham's descendants. So Abraham enlisted his chief household servant, presumably Eliezer, to carry out this task.

Why Abraham didn't send his son or go himself, we don't know. Maybe he was too old and unable to make such a trip, or perhaps it was because he knew if he left, he and/or his son might not want to return to the Promised Land. He'd been distracted before, so this might have been a possibility.

Before sending his servant on this journey, Abraham said to him, "Put your hand under my thigh." Searching for material on the significance of such an oath, I was surprised to find several sources indicate this was the closest place to the reproductive organs and hence, the solemn oath meant that it would bring certain obligations to keep the promise, at all costs, in order to protect the following generations.[1]

Abraham continued with further instruction to his servant, "I want you to swear by the Lord, the God of heaven and the God of earth, that you will not get a wife for my son from the daughters of the Canaanites, among whom I am living, but you will go to my country and my own relatives and get a wife for my son Isaac" (Genesis 24:3-4).

The servant then asked him, "What if the woman is unwilling to come back with me to this land? Shall I then take your son back to the country you came from?"

Abraham's answer was a resounding, "No." He said, "The Lord, the God of heaven, who brought me out of my father's household and my native land, who spoke to me and promised me saying, 'To your offspring I will give this land,' he will send this angel before you so that you can get a wife for my son from there. If the woman is unwilling to come back with you, then you will be released from this oath of mine" (Genesis 24:6-8).

So the servant put his hand under the thigh of his master Abraham and swore an oath to him concerning this matter (Genesis 24:9). This event represents how serious it is to take an oath. It meant that you were true to your word and you would do as you swore to do.

It used to be when a witness came to testify in court, he swore an oath on the Holy Bible to tell the truth. This meant that what came out of the witness's mouth would be heard not only by those in the courtroom, but by God; therefore, it would be the truth. That is no longer the case. Nowadays, a witness takes an oath to tell the truth, but not by any standard to which they are held, except maybe being fined or put in jail if they are found to have lied. It no longer has the same effect as swearing before the God of heaven and earth.

As Christians, we are admonished, even without taking an oath, not to lie to each other since we have taken off our old self, with its practices, and put on the new self, which is being renewed in knowledge in the image of its Creator (Colossians 3:9-10). Our word to our spouses, children, friends and colleagues should always be the truth. When we say we will do something, we need to do it. It not only shows that we keep our promises, but gives glory and honor to our Lord.

Thank you, Father, for Your holy word that teaches me the importance of keeping my word, not only to my loved ones, friends and acquaintances, but to You. Keep me ever mindful that when I asked Jesus to be the Lord and Savior in my life, I committed to a lifetime of service and honor to You. Help me to be a person of my word so that You will be glorified. In the name of Jesus, I pray. Amen.

DAY 58

ANSWERED PRAYER
Read Genesis 24:10-27

Not only did Abraham's servant make preparations for his long journey by taking camels and all kinds of good things, such as jewelry, clothing and other costly gifts, but he was filled with determination to carry out his oath for Abraham. He arrived in Nahor, the land of Abraham's family, near a well outside of town, where he had his camels kneel down. It was evening, the time that women came to draw water.

The first thing he did was pray, "O Lord, God of my master Abraham, give me success today and show kindness to my master Abraham. See, I am standing beside this spring and the daughters of the townspeople are coming out to draw water. May it be that when I say to a girl, 'Please let down your jar that I may have a drink,' and she says, 'Drink, and I will water your camels too,' let her be the one you have chosen for your servant Isaac. By this I will know that you have shown kindness to my master." Before he finished praying, Rebekah came out with her jar on her shoulder. She was very beautiful, a virgin; no man had ever slept with her (Genesis 24:11-16).

Abraham's servant asked Rebekah for some water and she quickly lowered the jar to her hands and gave him water to drink. Then she offered to draw water for his camels. Do you think he was having difficulty containing his excitement at this point? It is a beautiful thing when we pray and God sends an instant answer. It doesn't always happen that way, but when it does, oh my, what a blessing it is. Abraham's servant gives us a great lesson in being tactful. He doesn't blurt out to Rebekah why he is there and expect her to respond. He asks a favor of her, a drink of water, which begins a conversation between them.

I sometimes bemoan the fact that I have not personally led anyone to Christ, especially when I read and hear about those who have. I have learned it is not always about approaching someone the first time you meet and asking, "Are you saved?" Sometimes it takes getting to know someone and building a relationship of trust, allowing the Holy Spirit to work and produce the fruit. We may not know this side of heaven who will be there because of our kindness and words of comfort toward them. Paul wrote to the Corinthians about this very thing when he said, "I planted the seed, Apollos watered it, but God made it grow. So neither he who plants nor he who waters is anything, but only God, who makes things grow" (1 Corinthians 3:6-7).

Then he asked Rebekah, "Whose daughter are you? Please tell me, is there room in your father's house for us to spend the night?" She answered him, "I am the daughter of Bethuel, Nahor's son" (remember Genesis 22:20-24). She added, "We have plenty of straw and fodder, as well as room for you to spend the night." Then the man bowed down and worshiped the Lord saying, "Praise be to the Lord, the God of my master Abraham...As for me, the Lord has led me on the journey to the house of my master's relatives" (Genesis 24:23-27). What an example of a godly man who not only says a prayer before taking any action, but when his prayer is answered, he immediately bows down and worships the Lord, giving Him thanks and praise.

There are many scriptures in the Bible that speak to the importance of prayer. It would take pages and pages to mention them all. Prayer in the life of a Christian is so important that Jesus told His disciples a parable to show them that they should always pray and not give up (Luke 18:1). The Apostle Paul wrote to the Philippians about it as well saying, "Do not be anxious about anything but in everything, by prayer and petition, with thanksgiving, present your requests to God (Philippians 4:6). Then when we receive the answer to our prayers, we must remember to give thanks to the Lord, for He is good.

Heavenly Father, I rejoice in Your goodness. Thank You that when I pray, You hear my prayers. May I always trust that even when the answers don't come immediately or in the way I think they should that You are faithful. In the name of Jesus, I pray. Amen.

DAY 59

REBEKAH'S ANSWER
Read Genesis 24:28-58

What began as an ordinary day for Rebekah, who came to draw water at the well, ended in a decision that changed the course of her life. Imagine the emotions she must have experienced when a perfect stranger asked her for a drink of water and then told her she had been chosen by God to be the wife of his master's son; and that he knows this because of the prayer he just prayed. If this happened to any of us, what would we do, think or say?

Rebekah was so thrilled by what this man said, she ran home and told her mother's household about these things. When her brother heard the news, he hurried out to meet Abraham's servant, who was standing by his camels near the spring. He said (to the servant), "Why are you standing out here? I have prepared the house and a place for the camels." They went to the house and offered him food, but he refused to eat until he explained why he was there (Genesis 24:31-33).

The atmosphere in that home must have been electrifying as the servant spoke of his mission and how God answered his prayer. Laban, Rebekah's brother, and Bethuel, her father, answered, "This is from the Lord; we can say nothing to you one way or the other. Here is Rebekah, take her and go, and let her become the wife of your master's son, as the Lord has directed." When Abraham's servant heard what they said, he bowed down to the ground before the Lord (Genesis 24:50-51).

Notice how the Lord is mentioned in every decision by everyone involved. As believers in Christ, this is a wonderful example of how to react when we know that God is guiding us and answering our prayers.

Abraham's servant then blessed Rebekah and her family with the gifts he brought with him. There must have been quite the celebration that night as they ate and drank together. With no delay, the next morning it was back to business when Abraham's servant said, "Send me on my way to my master." There was some hesitancy on the part of Rebekah's family for her to leave so suddenly. They asked that she be allowed to remain with them for ten days, but he insisted and said to them, "Do not detain me, now that the Lord has granted success to my journey. Send me on my way so I may go to my master." They were still hesitant, and responded, "Let's call the girl and ask her about it." So they called Rebekah and asked her, "Will you go with this man?" "I will go," she said (Genesis 24:53-58).

Rebekah's response is a beautiful example of obedience. It must have been difficult for all involved to have such a drastic change in their family, but she knew that she was chosen by God. Her example is the standard we should follow when we know God has a calling on our life. There is no time to hesitate because we may lose our opportunity. Had she decided to stay with her family those ten days, who knows what might have happened. We don't have to wonder about that, because she did exactly what the Lord directed her to do. She went, and as we will see, she was blessed for it.

Lord God Almighty, thank You for the lives of those who have come before us, who through their actions have shown the way to righteousness and obedience. They too were far from perfect, just as we are, but when they answered the call, You blessed them. Help me to learn from them and know that when I do not hesitate when You call, You are always faithful in what You have promised. In the name of Jesus, I pray. Amen.

DAY 60

ISAAC AND REBEKAH
Read Genesis 24:59-67

What was Isaac thinking during all this time? He must have known about his father's servant being sent to find a wife. Was he anxious, impatient, worried? What we read in Scripture is that he was out in the field near his home one evening meditating. That's a serene picture of a man who knows that God has everything under control. We're not told what his prayer was, but during this quiet time with God, he looked up and saw camels approaching.

When Rebekah looked up and saw Isaac, she got down from her camel and asked the servant, "Who is that man in the field coming to meet us?" "He is my master," he told her. So she took her veil and covered herself, a sign of not only submission, but of humility and modesty. When they met, the servant told Isaac all he had done. Then Isaac brought Rebekah into the tent of his mother and he married her.

How old-fashioned, you might say. Or you might think: They

didn't even know each other yet; how could they do that? What, no engagement? Before judging history by today's standards, let's not forget that arranged marriages were not unusual back then. Let's also remember that this was a marriage arranged by God and, as such, it was holy, it was ordained and it was to fulfill His plan and purpose, not theirs. The romantic and touching part about this "arranged marriage" by God is we are told, "So she became his wife and he loved her."

Oh, they will have their challenges, as we shall see, but what marriage doesn't? This is why it is important to marry a believer in Christ Jesus, so that when challenges come, we have someone (Jesus) to go to for help. Marriage is a sacred commitment that is not to be taken lightly. It should be honored by all and the marriage bed kept pure (Hebrews 13:4). In this manner, we honor God, for He hates divorce. Has not the Lord made them one? In body and spirit they are His. And what does He want? Godly children from their union (Malachi 2:15-16, NLT).

Lord, for those of us who are older and have perhaps been married for a while, this may not seem like such an issue, but for young people in today's society, it certainly is. They are bombarded with many confusing ideas in the world about their sexuality, but I know Your Word leaves no question as to who they are in You. I pray right now, especially for those who are young and contemplating marriage, that they not only seek advice from people who are already married, but, most importantly, that they seek Your desire for their lives and end up with the partner they are best suited for. May they one day honor You as a witness to what a godly marriage can truly be. In the precious name of Jesus, I pray. Amen.

DAY 61

A DIVINE PATTERN
Re-read Genesis 24

After listening to sermons, doing research and being in prayer, I believe this is the appropriate place to expand on a 1960's sermon, "A Divine Pattern," preached by David Pawson.[1] His insight on this subject is so powerful, it is worth repeating in my own words. Though his sermon dates back to the late 1960s, it is still applicable this very moment. What a testimony to the Scripture which says that God never changes (Malachi 3:6).

A pattern is where it all begins when it comes to sewing, and that's how I think of this. When we take the pieces of paper for a pattern and cut them out, they begin to fit together but it's not until we buy the fabric, lay the pattern on it, cut it out and sew it that we get a finished product. In this instance, God is the creator of the pattern. Abraham, Abraham's servant, Isaac and Rebekah are the fabric, and the finished product is the knowledge we have that God worked everything out by His divine pattern and for His intended purpose.

Beginning with Isaac, we have a pattern of Christ. As he and his father Abraham were walking towards the place of sacrifice (Calvary), he most likely helped carry the wood (the cross), which was to be used in the process of his death. Though Isaac was rescued from this fate seconds before the knife came down, we mustn't forget Abraham who represents a pattern of God because he was willing to sacrifice the son of God's promise. We know that God did this for us (1 John 4:9-10) and that Jesus willingly laid down his life for us (1 John 3:16).

Then we have Abraham (God), who sent his servant (the Holy Spirit), on behalf of Isaac (Christ), to find Rebekah (the bride of Christ). The analogy of each person in the body to their spiritual counterpart shows how things that take place in the spiritual realm can come to fruition in the natural realm. When God created Adam and Eve, they were intended to live forever in His perfect garden. If they hadn't sinned against their Creator, we wouldn't be living in the world we live in today. Because they exercised their free will and did what pleased them instead of God, He had a plan, and that plan did not include them eating from the tree of life and living forever in their sin. Thank you, Jesus!

We, my sweet friends, are the recipients of all that is encompassed in God's word involving those who came before us. We have a complete picture of what it was like before Christ, what it was like at the time of Christ and what it will be like when He returns. Those like Abraham, Abraham's servant, Isaac and Rebekah tell this story over and over again. Can I hear a Hallelujah?

Lord, what a beautiful example of who You are as we read about the lives of Abraham, Abraham's servant, Isaac and Rebekah. Thank You that You have not left me alone with no guidance for how to live for You. May I never take for granted that which You have given me to read each and every day. May the words of my mouth and the meditations of my heart be pleasing in Your sight and draw me closer to You. In the name of Jesus, I pray. Amen.

DAY 62

THE DEATH OF ABRAHAM
Read Genesis 25:1-18

At one-hundred and seventy-five years old, Abraham breathed his last and died at a good age, an old man and "full of years." His life had meaning and purpose because he served the One True God and had faith. Surprisingly, though, we find out he married, presumably after Sarah died, a woman named Keturah and they had six sons.

This passage has puzzled me since the first time I read it. How could a man of faith like Abraham have all these children by different women when God spoke to him about having one heir from which his descendants, God's chosen people and eventually, the Savior of the world, would come?

After much searching, I still don't have an answer. There is speculation as to who Keturah was. Some even suggest she was Hagar with a name change. Maybe, but I'm thinking she was not. In 1 Chronicles 1:32, Keturah is referred to as Abraham's concubine, which could possibly mean she was a part of his life when Sarah was alive, and her children were born during that time. It was customary in those days for men to have both wives and concubines.

I guess we'll have to wait until we get to heaven to ask because the Bible does not elaborate. And though I firmly believe God's plan in marriage is for one man and one woman, we have no record of God either condoning or condemning Abraham's choices to have more than one wife and more than one son. Abraham had nothing except his faith. We have an entire Bible to read and learn from, a Bible which refers back to the life of Abraham, the friend of God, on many occasions.

So Abraham was buried by Ishmael and Isaac, in the field of Ephron, son of Zohar the Hittite, the field Abraham bought to bury Sarah, his wife. Ishmael is mentioned in this chapter, as are his 12 sons who were tribal rulers according to their settlements and camps. Other than saying they lived in hostility toward all their brothers, there is not much said as to who they are and where exactly they ended up living. Muslims believe Ishmael was a prophet and an ancestor of Muhammad.[1]

Many Arabs also believe they are Ishmael's descendants, which, if true, could explain why they live in hostility toward their brothers. That's the exact scenario in which we find ourselves today, conflict between the Jews and Arabs. Whoever these descendants were and are, they apparently were born, lived and died. The Bible says nothing of their accomplishments, if any. It was not worth noting when it came to God's story, for they neither believed in nor served the One True God.

Before he died, Abraham left everything to Isaac, though he also gave gifts to the sons of his concubines, sending them away from his son Isaac to the land of the east, leaving little chance that they would be able to lay claim to any of Isaac's inheritance. Abraham knew Isaac was the son of promise, so he blessed him accordingly and made him heir of his entire estate, including the Promised Land, even though it didn't yet belong to him.

This part of the story may not apply much to us today other

than as historical information about the latter years of Abraham, his sons and his death. What we do know is that Abraham was a man of God who, at the end of his life, knew Isaac was the chosen one and gave him everything. We also know that a life such as Ishmael's and his sons, though maybe they had great worldly wealth and accomplishments, did not gain favor with God. So we can once again ask the question: Are we an Isaac or an Ishmael—a person of faith or a person of the world?

Lord, I have come to passages in Your Word that seem so far removed from me that it's difficult to understand their significance to my life today. But I trust that they serve a purpose for teaching, rebuking, correcting, and training in righteousness so that I may be thoroughly equipped for every good work (2 Timothy 3:16). I thank You for this. In the name of Jesus, I pray. Amen.

DAY 63

DECEIT AND LIES; PROMISES AND BLESSINGS

Do not lie to each other, since you have taken off your old self with its practices and have put on the new self, which is being renewed in knowledge in the image of its Creator.
(Colossians 3:9-10)

Have you ever lied about something and then tried covering it up by telling another lie and then another lie? I have. When I was a teenager, I once begged my mom to go to a movie with my then boyfriend. She finally relented and, against her better judgment, let me go. Well, we decided to meet some friends at a pool hall instead, and we never made it to the movie. When I got home my mom asked, "How was the movie?" "Oh, it was okay. We had fun." Not knowing that she'd already seen the movie I told her we were going to, she asked, "What did you like best?" I had seen some previews, so I said something about the part I had seen. Then I told her I was tired and wanted to go to bed. She didn't say anything else until later when she came to my room and asked, "What did you really do tonight?"

My mind kind of went crazy. I thought she believed me and I was trying to think of another "believable" lie to tell her. I decided to just tell her the truth. It felt like a weight lifted off my chest because even though I knew there would be consequences, I couldn't deal with the feeling of lying about something I had no reason to lie about. When I told her, she wasn't as upset about where I had been as the fact I had lied to her. That was a life lesson I will never forget, which leads me to the rest of the story, as Paul Harvey would say, of Isaac.

Chapters 25-28 of Genesis continue the story of four people, Isaac, Rebekah, and their twin sons, Esau and Jacob. It's full of promises, prayers, blessings, stealing, deceit, and lying. Despite the good, the bad, the failings and the weaknesses, God accomplished His plans. As we will see along this journey, a great nation was born of Abraham, and they are still with us to this very day.

What can we learn from this? What I've learned is that it's better to be honest. However, when we do mess up, we can trust the Lord to not only forgive us, but help us do better. Just like my mom didn't stop loving me because I lied to her, the Lord never stops loving us. When we are tempted, He will always make a way for us not to yield to our temptations (1 Corinthians 10:13).

Heavenly Father, I'm so thankful for Your Word and its truth. I pray for strength and wisdom to make the right choices and to honor You always. In the name of Jesus, I pray. Amen.

DAY 64

ESAU AND JACOB
Read Genesis 25:19-26

There is a familiar refrain when we come to the marriage of Isaac and Rebekah. After almost 20 years of marriage, they had no children. Then Isaac prayed to the Lord on behalf of his wife because she was barren. The Lord answered his prayer, and his wife Rebekah became pregnant. There's no mention of Isaac having concubines or other children, which makes for a lot less family drama, at least until the children are grown.

Isaac is a man of prayer who cares deeply about his wife and her needs, and so he prays to God for her. Imagine if husbands prayed for their wives when they had a need, or even when they didn't. It may not be for a child, but as a husband, he should have such an intimate relationship with his wife that he knows what prayers she needs. We know that Isaac's prayer was answered by God, giving good reason to believe the prayers of a godly man for his wife will also be answered.

It wasn't an easy pregnancy as the two babies jostled each other within her. Rebekah was so concerned about this she inquired of the Lord, "Why is this happening to me?" (Genesis 25:22). It's always a good thing to go to the Lord when we are struggling with something.

The Lord said to Rebekah, "Two nations are in your womb, and the two peoples from within you will be separated; one people will be stronger than the other and the older will serve the younger" (Genesis 25:23). Rebekah received her answer, although she may not have fully understood its implications at the time. The two did, indeed, become two nations; one representing human nature and the world (Esau), and the other representing the spirit and the kingdom of God (Jacob, whose name was later changed to Israel).

The boys grew up and Esau became a skillful hunter, a man of the open country, while Jacob was a quiet man, staying among the tents. Isaac, who had a taste for wild game, loved Esau, but Rebekah loved Jacob. This statement is telling in that it may be one among many reasons for the sibling rivalry between Esau and Jacob. They were so different from each other, it's hard to imagine that they were twins and each parent loved one of them more than the other. As the oldest of six children, I can speak from experience that it's best for parents not to show favoritism. It's difficult enough to get a parent's love and affection with that many children, but it can definitely create jealousy and hard feelings if one child feels less loved than another.

It seems as though the lives of these two brothers were on totally opposite paths and makes me wonder if they even had affection for one another. Esau was gone a lot of the time; Jacob was close to home. There was an occasion when the two were together. Jacob was cooking some stew when Esau came in from the open country. He said to Jacob, "Quick, let me have some of that red stew! I'm famished!" Jacob replied, "First, sell me your birthright." "Look, I am about to die," Esau said. "What good is the birthright to me?" But before Jacob would give his brother some stew, he made him swear an oath that he would sell his birthright. So, for some bread and lentil stew, Esau sold his birthright, which we are told he despised, fulfilling what the Lord said to Rebekah about the older serving the younger (Genesis 25:29-34). Jacob was determined from the time he came out of the womb holding his brother's heel that he was going to be first.

Like Ishmael and Isaac, we are given another example of human nature versus the spirit. Esau, the firstborn who should have been heir to the promise by tradition, was outwitted by his brother to give that right up, and he didn't even care. He wanted what he wanted right at the moment, not considering the consequences of his desire for immediate gratification. Jacob, waiting patiently and seizing the moment, by sheer determination got what he desperately wanted.

In today's society, instant gratification is the name of the game. We don't want to wait in line for anything, and we don't have to. One click of a mouse and Amazon has your purchase at your door in a day or two. Talk to Alexa and she can turn the stove on, change the temperature in the house, turn the lights on, among other things, and we don't even have to be home. Hard work is getting to be a thing of the past in some sectors of life.

There is much we can garner from what took place in the lives of these four people. Like families today, their family had challenges. When they sought God, prayers were answered. When they looked to do things their own way, it resulted in sibling rivalry and favoritism. Let's take that to heart and learn from their mistakes.

Lord, teach me to wait patiently for You when I am looking for answers. Help me especially in my family relations to look to You when difficulties arise that I see no answers for. There are many families in this world who are struggling, yet don't go to You in prayer. When the going gets tough, they walk away. Help my family to be the family of God You intend so that we honor you and are an example to those who are looking for answers. In the name of Jesus, I pray. Amen.

DAY 65

ISAAC AND ABIMELECH
Read Genesis 26:1-18

Isaac's life in chapter 26 is almost a mirror image of his father's. He left the land where he was because of famine and ended up in the land of the Philistines, a place called Gerar. Apparently his intent was to go to Egypt as his father had done. However, when the Lord spoke to him and said, "Do not go down to Egypt; live in the land where I tell you stay," he stayed put. At that time, God told Isaac he would be heir to the same promises as his father Abraham, if he obeyed (Genesis 26:1-6). He did obey, which is somewhat troubling when we come to the next thing that takes place.

It seems the men in Gerar took a liking to Isaac's wife because he became afraid and thought, "The men of this place might kill me on account of Rebekah, because she is beautiful." So, like father like son, Isaac lied about Rebekah being his wife and said she was his sister. Unlike Sarah, she apparently wasn't taken into Abimelech's harem or given to someone to be their wife because after they had been in the land a long time, Abimelech saw them together when looking down from a window and Isaac was caressing his wife. Abimelech summoned Isaac and said, "She is really your wife! Why did you say 'She is my sister'?" Isaac explained his dilemma and Abimelech gave him a harsh rebuke, but then ordered his people not to molest either Isaac or Rebekah, or they would be put to death (Genesis 26:7-11).

Lying always gets us in deeper trouble than if we told the truth from the beginning. Fortunately, Isaac came clean when confronted, but it had to have broken any bond of trust that existed between him and Abimelech, as it does for us when we lie. It takes a long time to rebuild trust once broken. It's not worth the lie in the long run. Especially as God's people we are told, "Do not lie to one another since you have taken off your old self with its practices and put on the new self which is being renewed in knowledge in the image of its Creator" (Colossians 3:9-10).

Isaac remained in the land and prospered greatly, so much so that the Philistines envied him, which ultimately led Abimelech to tell Isaac to "move away from us because you have become too powerful" (Genesis 26:16). Isaac then moved to the Valley of Gerar where disputes also arose. Being a quiet man and wanting to avoid confrontation he apparently packed up and continued moving, digging and unplugging wells wherever he went, until he dug a third well which no one quarreled over, naming it "Rehoboth," saying, "Now the Lord has given us room and we will flourish" (Genesis 26:22).

Tracing Isaac's journey, it seems all the disputes and quarreling actually led him to the place where the Lord wanted him to be, ending up in Beersheba, where God appeared to him. There, Isaac's life took a major turn. God said, "I am the God of your father Abraham. Do not be afraid, for I am with you; I will bless you and will increase the number of your descendants for the sake of my servant Abraham." Isaac built an altar there and called on the name of the Lord. He then pitched a tent and dug a well (Genesis 26:23-33).

Isaac finally came to the place where he trusted God completely, finding peace in knowing he had come to the place where God wanted him. After realizing this, he pitched his tent and then dug a well. He was now putting God first, which is a wonderful example for us to follow in our own walk with the Lord. When we seek first His kingdom, He provides our needs (Matthew 6:33).

Lord, check me in my spirit if I am ever tempted to lie. May I always be truthful in my dealings with others, remembering to seek first Your kingdom above all else. In the name of Jesus, I pray. Amen.

DAY 66

A SWORN AGREEMENT, AGAIN
Read Genesis 26:19-35

When Abimelech showed up sometime later, Isaac wasn't too impressed with his arrival and asked him, "Why have you come to me, since you were hostile to me and sent me away?" I probably would have asked the same question if I'd been told to leave the place where I had become quite wealthy and prospered greatly, then had to pick up and leave because of envy and jealousy. Abimelech's answer is telling when he says, "We saw clearly that the Lord was with you; so we said, 'There ought to be a sworn agreement between us'" (Genesis 26:27-31). They were looking for a mutual agreement between them to not harm each other, and Isaac was okay with that.

This may be an example of what Jesus told us to do when He said, "Love your enemies and pray for those who persecute you, that you may be sons of your Father in heaven" (Matthew 5:44). I wouldn't say Abimelech was necessarily an enemy, but he certainly wasn't an ally up to that time. The best thing is to always pray for the Lord's guidance and direction when it comes to these types of matters in our lives. Not that we will ever be in a position to sign an agreement with someone who at one time was unfriendly to us, but there are many aspects of life to which this could apply. And remember, when others see those who live a life for Christ, they see something different than what the world has to offer, and, who knows, one day that may lead to their salvation.

Isaac prepared a feast for them and early the next morning the men swore an oath to each other. Isaac sent them away, and they left in peace. That very day Isaac was blessed when his servants came and told him about a well that they dug saying, "We have found water!" It's in our obedience to Him that we are blessed.

The next paragraph gives us a tale of woe when we learn that Esau, at 40 years old, married two Hittite women. They were a source of grief to Isaac and Rebekah. Why? They were not of the faith, and this always leads to disruption in families and marriages. Isaac and Rebekah may have been the most godly parents in the world, but that doesn't mean their children followed in their footsteps. It took many years for Isaac to get out from under his own father's shadow and mistakes to come to a place he understood what it meant to be in a relationship with the Lord at a personal level. Abraham couldn't do that for him, and he couldn't do it for his son Esau.

Lord, thank You once again for blessing me with the Scriptures. No matter the naysayers, this is the Book of books that gives me guidance for how to live by learning from those who have come before me. And though it is not a history book of the world, it is Your history of Your people, and their faithfulness to You, though they were far from perfect. May I learn from their mistakes and become a more faithful follower of Christ because of what I am learning. In the precious name of Jesus, I pray. Amen.

DAY 67

BLESSING THROUGH DECEPTION
Read Genesis 27:1-40

There are few twin brothers more different from each other than Esau and Jacob. Esau, the outdoors and woodsy guy, was on the hunt, always looking for excitement. Jacob stayed close to home, a mama's boy, learning how to cook and keep the home fires burning. The fact that Isaac and Rebekah had their favorites didn't help.

When Isaac was old and his eyes were weak so he could no longer see, he called Esau, wanting to give him a blessing. But first he asked Esau, "Prepare me the kind of tasty food I like and bring it to me to eat, so that I may give you my blessing before I die."

Why Isaac needed a meal before giving the blessing is not certain, but it sure opened up a door of opportunity for his other son. Rebekah was listening in on this conversation and came up with a plan. While Esau was hunting, she instructed Jacob to bring two choice young goats so she could prepare tasty food for his father the way he liked it. Then, she told Jacob to take it to his father so he could receive the blessing.

Jacob was afraid his father would know it was him and instead of being blessed, he would be cursed. However, Rebekah had a ready-made answer, "My son, let the curse fall on me. Just do what I say." Rebekah not only prepared the food, but she took the best clothes of Esau and put them on Jacob. Then she covered his hands and the smooth part of his neck with the goatskins, as Esau was a hairy man, and Jacob went to his father. It is as though she had been preparing all along for this very opportunity.

Jacob was surprised that his son returned so quickly with the meal but Jacob assured him that, "The Lord your God gave me success." Then Isaac said, "Come near so I can touch you my son, to know whether you are really my son Esau." When Jacob came near, Isaac touched him and said, "The voice is the voice of Jacob but the hands are the hands of Esau." So Isaac blessed him.

I never understood why Rebekah did this. While the twins were still in her womb, God told her that the older would serve the younger. Since she knew that, why didn't she have enough faith to believe it would work out instead of deceiving her own husband and causing her son to lie to his father? Then again, why did Isaac secretly call Esau to receive a blessing without letting Rebekah and Jacob know about it? That's sometimes how families are, aren't they? How many secrets lie at the root of family chaos and bitterness? Or how many times have we gone ahead of the Lord because we didn't want to wait for Him to answer in His timing, or because we wanted a different outcome than what we knew God planned? If we don't do things God's way, there is always strife, especially when lying is involved.

When Esau returned to his father he was shocked to hear him ask, "Who are you?" "I am your son," said Esau, "your firstborn, Esau." Isaac trembled violently – he must have been so angry – and he said, "Who was it then that hunted game and brought it to me? I ate it just before you came and I blessed him, and indeed he will be blessed!" Can you hear the gut-wrenching voice of Esau as he slid across the floor on his knees and with a loud, bitter cry said to his father, "Bless me – me too, my father!" Isaac said to him, "Your brother came deceitfully and took your blessing." Esau should have let dead dogs lie, so to speak, but he insisted, "Do you have only one blessing, my father? Bless me too, my father!" Isaac answered him, "Your dwelling will be away from the earth's richness, away from the dew of heaven above. You will live by the sword and you will serve your brother. But when you grow restless, you will throw his yoke from your neck" (Genesis 27:30-40). That sounds more like a curse than a blessing, but Esau insisted and that's what he received.

Here is a family of God torn apart because Isaac's wife, like Abraham's wife Sarah, didn't wait upon the Lord, but came up with her own solution for what she perceived was a problem. What must the Lord have thought during all of the drama that was taking place? Nothing is said about any of them consulting or praying to the Lord about any of it.

Waiting is not something we are very good at these days. I know I get impatient when things don't happen as quickly as I think they should. However, those who wait upon the Lord shall renew their strength; they shall mount up with wings as eagles; they shall run and not be weary; they shall walk and not faint (Isaiah 40:31). If we wait upon Him, He will renew our strength, keep us from becoming weary and we will not faint. Those are blessings worth waiting for.

Lord, help me to not look for the easy way around things, which often results in lying and deceit to get intended results. May I always call upon You for strength to be truthful in everything I think, do and say, so that You will be honored and I will be in peace. In the name of Jesus, I pray. Amen.

DAY 68

JACOB FLEES
Read Genesis 27:41 - 28:9

If Rebekah and Jacob knew how serious the consequences of their deceit and trickery would be, maybe they would have thought more clearly about what they were doing. Like most sinful acts, we often do not think about that until it is too late. Esau was so angry, the grudge he held against his brother began to boil like a hot caldron and he said to himself, "The days of mourning for my father are near; then I will kill my brother Jacob" (Genesis 27:41).

Somehow Rebekah got wind of this and instructed Jacob to flee at once to her brother Laban for a time. Unfortunately, for both of them, this became more than a short separation. It would be 20 years before Jacob returned, and it appears he and Rebekah never saw each other again. How heartbreaking.

Before sending Jacob off, Rebekah complained bitterly to her husband, "I am disgusted with living because of these Hittite women (referring to those Esau had married). If Jacob takes a wife from among the women of this land... my life will not be worth living" (Genesis 27:46). It was a dramatic urging for Isaac to do something.

This time Isaac called Jacob of his own accord, possibly feeling he had no choice if he wanted to please his wife. He blessed him again, sending him away with a commandment to take a wife from among the daughters of Laban, his mother's brother. He added to his blessing by saying, "May God Almighty bless you and keep you and make you fruitful and increase your numbers until you become a community of peoples. May He give you and your descendants the blessing given to Abraham, so that you may take possession of the land where you now live as an alien, the land God gave to Abraham." Then Isaac sent him away (Genesis 28:1-5).

When Esau learned of this additional blessing on Jacob by his father, he realized how displeasing the Canaanite (Hittite) women were to his father Isaac. So he married one of Ishmael's daughters, in addition to the wives he already had. Sadly, it was too little too late to please his father by marrying one of Abraham's granddaughters. Even though she was a daughter of Ishmael, the son born to Hagar, she was not the heir of Abraham's covenant with God. When we try making things right by our own efforts, excluding any thought of God in our decisions, it still does not bring a blessing from Him, something which Esau apparently did not understand.

Wow, that is a lot to absorb, isn't it? It has all the elements of intrigue needed for a movie, but this is real life. It actually happened, and these are God's people! As Robert Deffinbaugh of the Community Bible Chapel in Richardson, Texas said in a sermon on Esau and Jacob, "Man's sin can never frustrate the will of God, but it can fulfill it." Adding, "The sins of Isaac, Esau, Rebekah and Jacob did not in any way thwart God's will from being done."[1] His will was that the children of promise were to come through Jacob, not Esau. Rebekah knew this before her sons were born.

This doesn't mean that God condones sin, but, as we will hear from someone greatly wronged by his own brothers later in Genesis, "...what you meant for evil against me, God meant for good" (Genesis 50:20). God's divine plans and purposes will never be thwarted by someone's sins of lie and deceit (Galatians 6:7).

Lord, I don't want to live in a world of lies and deceit, but that is exactly where I am. Help me to remain faithful all the days of my life so that, as You promised in the letter written by Paul to the Colossians, I will be without blemish and free from accusation, if I continue in my faith, because of the precious blood of Jesus that washes away all of my sins. Amen.

DAY 69

JACOB'S DREAM
Read Genesis 28:10-22

How must Jacob have felt as he fled everything he ever knew and began a journey in the wilderness? Was he feeling regret over having deceived his father and betraying his brother? Was he angry with his mother for devising such a plan that went awry? Was he feeling alone and forsaken, not knowing what to expect when he arrived at his uncle's home? He was human, so it's not far-fetched that it was a very emotional time for him. At some point along the way he got tired. When he reached a certain place, he stopped for the night because the sun set. Taking one of the stones there, he put it under his head and laid down to sleep (Genesis 28:10-11).

Then Jacob had a dream in which he saw a stairway resting on the earth, with its top reaching to heaven, and the angels of God were ascending and descending on it. There above it stood the Lord who said to Jacob, "I am the Lord, the God of your father Abraham and the God of Isaac. I will give your descendants the land on which you are lying. Your descendants will be like the dust of the earth and you will spread out to the west and to the east, to the north and to the south. All peoples on earth will be blessed through you and your offspring. I am with you and will watch over you and your offspring...and I will bring you back to this land. I will not leave you until I have done what I have promised to you" (Genesis 28:11-15).

That is some dream. Jacob thought so, and when he awoke from his sleep, perhaps for the first time in his life he thought, "Surely the Lord is in this place and I was not aware of it" (Genesis 28:16). This seems to be the ah-hah moment for Jacob, when for the first time he hears directly from God that his descendants are the ones through whom all peoples on earth will be blessed and that one day God will bring him back to this land.

When was your ah-hah moment when you realized you couldn't do life any longer without Jesus? I remember mine. A friend invited me to church, and though I could not tell you what the sermon was about, I was moved by the Spirit of God to ask Jesus to come into my heart and forgive me of my sins. My life has never been the same since. Neither was Jacob's life ever the same. We are never the same once we have been touched by God.

Though Jacob was afraid, he said, "How awesome is this place! This is none other than the house of God; this is the gate to heaven." Then he set up a pillar and poured oil on top of it to mark the exact place. He called the place Bethel, meaning "the house of God," from its previous name of Luz, meaning "almond tree" (Genesis 28:17-19). Have you noticed a pattern here, that every time someone has an encounter with God, there is a name change, like Abram to Abraham, Sarai to Sarah, now Luz to Bethel. It's a life-changing experience to come into the presence of the Living God.

Once we experience God's presence, our lives don't magically become carefree and less burdensome. However, there is a new hope, a new trust, a new relationship with our Savior that leads us along the way to a better life in Him, the ultimate destination being eternal life. Therefore, it should not be difficult, as Peter wrote, "to rid ourselves of all malice and all deceit, hypocrisy, envy and slander of every kind. Like newborn babies, we should crave pure spiritual milk so that by it we may grow up in our salvation, now that we have tasted that the Lord is good" (1 Peter 2:1-3).

Then Jacob made a vow, saying, "If God will be with me and will watch over me on this journey I am taking and will give me food to eat and clothes to wear so that I return safely to my father's house, then the Lord will be my God..." (Genesis 28:20-21). That's what happens when Jesus enters into our hearts; the Spirit of God becomes our guide and we have a desire to please only Him, to pray and ask for His will and not our own; and we also have the knowledge that He is always with us and we can trust Him with our very lives.

Lord, thank You again for giving me Your word so that I am able to read about those who came before me. They were far from perfect, as am I, yet You saw them where they were and You called them to You. May You do the same for me when I cry out to You. In the holy and precious name of Jesus, I pray. Amen.

DAY 70

ALL IN THE FAMILY
Read Genesis 29:1-14

The first time I shared "my testimony" with a friend, I told her it felt like a ton of bricks was lifted off my shoulders, and I wasn't kidding. I remember feeling like someone literally came down from heaven and physically lifted a multitude of bricks off my shoulders. Bricks that I had no idea were there until they were gone.

There is no way I can know how Jacob was feeling as he continued his journey to Haran, but I would venture to say he might have been walking with his head a little higher, maybe even a bounce in his step, than when he began. He also might have had no idea what he was facing when he arrived, but somehow it didn't matter. God was with him.

Jacob came to the land of the eastern peoples and there he saw a well in the field. He saw shepherds who were tending their flocks and asked them,

"My brothers, where are you from?"

"We're from Haran," they answered.

"Do you know Laban, Nahor's grandson?"

"Yes, we know him."

"Is he well?"

"Yes, he is," they said, "and here comes his daughter Rachel with the sheep" (Genesis 29:4-6).

It's interesting that Jacob ended up at a well as he was on his way to find a wife, like Abrahams' servant who went looking for a wife for Isaac. The first woman he saw was Laban's daughter, whom he later married. However, as we will learn, the way he gets there is nothing like the marriage of Isaac and Rebekah.

Apparently, the shepherds whom Jacob just met were waiting around the well for someone to roll the stone away so that all of the flocks could be watered at the same time. When Jacob saw Rachel, he went over, rolled the stone away from the mouth of the well and watered his uncle's sheep. He was so excited to be there, learning that his uncle was well, that he kissed Rachel and began to weep aloud. Then he told Rachel who he was, and she ran home to tell her father.

As soon as Laban received the news, he hurried to meet Jacob. He embraced him, kissed him and brought him to his home. Jacob told him why he was there, though it's doubtful he explained the trickery that he and his mother played on his father. Laban said to him, "You are my own flesh and blood." They must have gotten to know each other pretty well because Jacob stayed with Laban for an entire month before they got down to business (Genesis 29:9-14).

For the first time in a while, it sounds like one big happy family, right? Jacob is greeted with open arms as part of the family and all seems well. However, outward appearances are not always an indication of what is really going on, because trouble was stirring that would take years for Jacob to discover.

Many families, including Christian families, struggle with similar issues. We want others to think everything is just fine, when often it is not. We don't have to shout it from the rooftops, but we can be open and honest, and go to our Father in prayer about what is going on. And if we know that He hears us (and He does), whatever we ask, we know that we have what we asked of Him (1 John 5:15).

Lord, teach me to pray earnestly when I am in need. Help me not to pretend problems don't exist just because I want others to think I have it all together. I hurt, Lord, and I struggle in my relationships, and I need help to figure it out. Thank You that You are with me and that You do hear me when I pray. In the name of Jesus, I pray. Amen.

DAY 71

JACOB DECEIVED
Read Genesis 29:15-30

One thing about doing research for a devotional on the Old Testament is there are many sources for research and opinions, so many that it gets overwhelming and confusing. There is a majority of agreement on good portions of scripture, but when it came to Laban, Jacob, Leah and Rachel, it was all over the place. So I've been spending some time in prayer, asking for direction on what we can glean from what took place in this passage in Genesis 29:15-30. Here it goes.

After a month's time, Laban said to Jacob, "Just because you are a relative of mine should you work for me for nothing? Tell me what your wages should be?" Apparently Jacob had been giving Laban free labor, but it also gave him a chance to get to know Rachel better. Jacob answered Laban, "I'll work for you seven years in return for your younger daughter Rachel" (Genesis 29:15-18).

This is in stark contrast to Isaac and Rebekah. When

Abraham sent his servant out to find a wife for Isaac, he came prepared with many gifts and supplies to give to Rebekah's family, and once the decision was made that Rebekah would go, she and Isaac were married immediately. Jacob, on the other hand, left home with nothing. He had no support from his father, either financially or emotionally, when it came to choosing a wife. He had no dowry, and the only thing he could offer was his labor in return for a wife.

When the seven years were up, there was a big celebration. Jacob was prepared to receive his wife. Unbeknownst to him, Laban gave his oldest daughter, Leah, instead of Rachel, which Jacob discovered the next morning. Scripture says Leah had "weak eyes" (Genesis 29:17). The Hebrew word for "weak" here actually means "tender" or "delicate."[1] Perhaps she was more of the quiet type, much less assertive than her younger sister, but not necessarily homely or difficult to look upon.

Though obviously distressed when he discovered Laban's deceit, the marriage had been consummated and Leah was now Jacob's wife. However, Jacob loved Rachel, so he agreed to work seven additional years for her. After a week with Leah, Laban gave Rachel to Jacob, and he worked an additional seven years for Laban (Genesis 29:25-28).

Once we do something, good or bad, we can never go back and change it, and there are always consequences. Had Rebekah and Jacob not conspired to trick Isaac, God would have made the way for Jacob to receive the blessing of the firstborn. Instead of having to run away, Jacob may have had his father's blessing in regard to choosing a wife, as well as financial stability to take care of her without having to work for someone else. If so, then he never would have been deceived by his father-in-law to take both of his daughters in marriage. These are all "what ifs," so we will never know what God's original plan was. What we do know is that God did not take his blessing from Jacob and that, though Jacob loved Rachel more than Leah, it was Leah through whom the lineage of Jesus continued, not Rachel.

One thing we can garner from this story is that honesty is always the best policy. This story would have been different had there been honesty. Let's learn from these lessons and apply it to our lives today. When we find ourselves thinking there's a better way than God's way, it's a good time to step back and consider the consequences of lying or deceiving someone to get what we want. It just isn't worth the heartache that follows. God's way is always best.

Lord, help me to always be honest with You, with myself and with others. When there are times I am doubtful which way to turn, I ask for guidance to know the choice that honors You. In the precious name of Jesus, I pray. Amen.

DAY 72

JACOB'S CHILDREN
Read Genesis 29:31-30:24

One person who is often overlooked in this story is Leah. Imagine how she must have felt knowing that when they awoke in the morning, Jacob would discover it was not Rachel and she would be spurned by her husband. She had fortitude, though, and didn't wallow in her sorrow, but took full advantage of being Jacob's first wife.

After her first son, she said, "It is because the Lord has seen my misery. Surely my husband will love me now." She had a longing, a desire, to be loved by her husband. Wouldn't you? It's not often one has to contend for the love of one's husband with your own sister, but that was the situation.

She conceived again and when she gave birth she said, "Because the Lord heard that I am not loved, He gave me this one too." Then a third time, "Now at last my husband will become attached to me because I have borne him three sons." When she gave birth to a fourth son she said, "This time I will praise the Lord." Then she stopped having children (Genesis 29:31-35).

Leah must have felt great disappointment that the birth of their sons did not bring her husband to her side. She eventually overcame that disappointment by giving praise to the Lord.

Meanwhile, Rachel was barren and she became jealous of her sister, demanding of her husband, "Give me children, or I'll die!" Jacob became angry at her and said, "Am I in the place of God who has kept you from having children?" (Genesis 30:1-2).

History repeats itself in that, like Sarah, Rachel being unable to have children, gave Jacob her concubine by which to have children, and she had two. When Leah realized she couldn't have any more children, she gave Jacob her concubine, and she had two children. The two sisters get into an argument. Leah gets what she wants, which is time with Jacob. They have two more sons, plus a daughter (Genesis 30:3-21).

Up to this point, Leah is the only one praying to God, and He listened to her. She had her fifth son and said, "God has rewarded me for giving my maidservant to my husband." When the sixth son came, she said, "God has presented me with a precious gift. This time my husband will treat me with honor because I have borne him six sons."

It seems as though Rachel had a change of attitude and began praying to God, because God remembered Rachel and opened her womb. When her son Joseph was born, she said, "God has taken away my disgrace. May the Lord add to me another son," which eventually He did (Genesis 30:22-24). So Jacob had 12 sons in all, and at least one daughter that we know of.

The person we can learn from the most in this story is Leah. She had a constant rivalry with her sister because Jacob loved Rachel, and Leah longed to be loved by her husband as well. She was disappointed that her husband did not love her, even after bearing sons to him, but she overcame her disappointment through prayer and praise.

How will we react when the one we love doesn't love us back? Will we remain disappointed and have a pity-party, or will we seek God and praise Him? God will never disappoint us, but He will always love us, for God is love, and whoever lives in love lives in God and God in him (1 John 4:16).

Lord, there are times I will disappoint others and they will disappoint me, but no matter what, may I always look to You for my source of true love and comfort. In the name of Jesus, I pray. Amen.

DAY 73

JACOB'S FLOCK INCREASES
Read Genesis 30:25 - 31:2

Fourteen years passed since Jacob arrived in Haran. He'd been a hard worker but it appears his wages were not enough to provide for his two wives, two concubines and 11 sons. So Jacob went to Laban asking to be sent on his way with his family. "Not so quick," Laban said. "I've been really blessed since you arrived. I don't want you to leave. How about you tell me what I can give you?" By this time Jacob must have known Laban wasn't always on the up and up and most likely had given some thought as to what he would do if Laban insisted he stay. "Don't give me anything," Jacob replied. "But if you do this one thing for me, I will go on tending your flocks and watching over them" (Genesis 30:25-31).

Once Jacob revealed his plan to remove all the speckled sheep and goats, as well as dark colored lambs, Laban must have thought he got the better deal because he agreed. Laban even went out that same day and removed all of the streaked and spotted male goats, all the speckled and spotted female goats and the dark colored lambs. Then Laban sent Jacob and his family on a three-day journey with them to separate himself from Jacob, though Jacob continued to tend the rest of Laban's flocks (Genesis 30:32-36).

By this time Jacob knew the flocks and their habits quite well. He'd been taking care of them for fourteen years and most likely tended sheep for his father before that, and he had a plan. He took fresh-cut branches from different trees and made white stripes on them by peeling the bark and exposing the white inner wood of the branches. Then he placed them directly in front of the flocks when they came to drink. When the stronger females of the flocks were in heat, they mated in front of the branches; the weaker animals he placed elsewhere. After the young of the stronger animals were born, they were streaked and speckled and spotted and Jacob set them apart for himself. After a time, Jacob grew exceedingly prosperous and came to own large flocks, maidservants, menservants, camels and donkeys. Laban was pretty upset about this change of events and his attitude toward Jacob changed (Genesis 30:37-31:2).

Life often gives us lemons when we're looking for sweet, ripened oranges. Maybe we've been in a job where our boss has taken advantage of us, or a co-worker asked for help on a project and then took full credit for it. Like Jacob, we might feel unappreciated and taken advantage of; but also like Jacob, we do not need to become bitter. A job change may not be possible, but a change of our hearts is. Scripture tells us to work as though working for the Lord, not for men since we know that we have an inheritance that we will receive from the Lord (Colossians 3:23). Jacob did, and God blessed him. It doesn't mean we will be prosperous in this world, but there's no question we will be with Jesus in the next (Luke 23:43). The thing is, if we have been wronged somehow, God remains faithful. He sees everything that everyone does, and anyone who does wrong will be repaid for his wrong, and there is no favoritism (Colossians 3:25).

Lord, Your story is so awesome. You have included the life stories of men and women who were just like us with the same trials and hardships, all imperfect yet some made perfect in You. I am also a work in progress, Lord, that's for sure. Take me like the potter; make and mold me until I am conformed into the image and likeness of our Savior, in whose name, I pray. Amen.

DAY 74

JACOB FLEES FROM LABAN
Read Genesis 31:1-18

The time came for Jacob to go back to his own country. He had no doubt about it when the Lord said to him, "Go back to the land of your fathers and to your relatives, and I will be with you" (Genesis 31:3). I'll pause right here to say, wow, if only I'd heard a message like that from God, then maybe I wouldn't have stayed away from my family as long as I did. However, there's no going back, and I know that.

If we have regrets about our decisions, we get stuck there, like a car in a ditch, and God can't use us until we deal with what's preventing us from moving forward. He does show us the things that get us stuck, and when He does, it's up to us to do something about it, and Jacob did.

He knew he'd fallen out of favor with Laban, so he sent word to his wives to come to the field where the flocks were and he instructed them to get ready to leave; it was time. As Jacob was explaining the situation to his wives, we learn more about Laban and Jacob's relationship. We even learn that it was God who provided the speckled, spotted and streaked animals, so as to take away Laban's livestock and give them to Jacob. God earlier showed Jacob in a dream that this is what He would do. The wives seemed to have had it with their father as well, feeling used and abused, and ready to take advantage of their husband's good fortune. The only thing is, this time Jacob didn't ask Laban; he just packed up all he owned and began the journey back to his father Isaac in the land of Canaan (Genesis 31:4-21). Was he afraid? Was he excited? What kind of emotions must he have been feeling after all this time?

Reconciliation is difficult, especially when you've been gone as long as Jacob was. I know. I was separated from my family for over 30 years before seeking reconciliation, and we're still trying to figure it out to this day. Still, it is not difficult with God, for "if anyone is in Christ, he is a new creation; the old has gone, the new has come! All this is from God who reconciled us to Himself through Christ and gave us the ministry of reconciliation: that God was reconciling the world to Himself in Christ, not counting men's sins against them" (2 Corinthians 5:17-19).

Isn't that amazing? Once we were separated from God because of our sins, but now, thank you Jesus, we are reconciled because of what Christ did for us on the cross. What greater gift can God give us than that!

Lord, thank You for the gift of reconciliation with You. I rejoice in what You have done for me, so thankful that I no longer have to live in my sinful ways, far away from you and lost in this world without hope. Teach me each day how to be better equipped to share the good news of Jesus Christ with others so they too may have reconciliation with you. In His precious name we pray. Amen.

DAY 75

RACHEL TAKES LABAN'S HOUSEHOLD GODS
Read Genesis 31:19

Why would Rachel steal her father's household gods? This one sentence in Genesis has puzzled me every time I've read it. I never think much about the personalities of the people we read about in the Old Testament. I just look at them as either followers of God or not, and those I consider unfaithful, I didn't care too much for. I missed important truths by doing that because each person teaches us things about ourselves when we identify with them in the history of time. They are important to the foundation of our faith because we can relate to them as human beings. They had thoughts, emotions and reasons for doing things, just like we do.

This is one of many reasons why I began this Old Testament devotional. I have learned so much through my research and studies, but most of all, it has drawn me closer to the Lord.

The Word of God is His Story to us. We often hear it said that we all have a story. Well, so does God, and He wants to share it with us. We are a blessed generation to not only have His written Word, but to also have more research on more subjects at the click of a mouse than we could ever consume in a lifetime. This is why I try to limit what I read once there seems to be a consistent theme on an issue or subject for which I am doing research.

Rachel was a little on the crafty side. Jacob loved her the most, and she knew it. She felt confident in their relationship and took full advantage of her position as Jacob's wife by antagonizing her older sister and deceiving her father. She knew taking her father's gods would upset him, but she did it anyway, telling no one. These household gods were often small statues of a family's ancestors. They were not necessarily worshiped by those who kept them, but they often were included in the inheritance and always went to the man of the house .

Her purpose in taking them could have been because she knew she would never return to her home again, nor see her father or relatives, and wanted something important to remember them by. Or perhaps she just didn't want her father to have them. I lean a little more toward the former because she chose to take them with her. If the latter were the case, she could have destroyed or buried them. Either way, they were not hers to take and she knew this. Had it been discovered she was the one who took them, there would have been serious repercussions, including death.

Being deceitful, as we learn time and time again, is not God's way. He never deceives. He never lies (Hebrews 6:18). So this might be a good place to stop for inner reflection, spending time with the Lord and asking Him, "Lord, see if there is any offensive way in me, and lead me in the way everlasting" (Psalm 139:24).

We know when we are doing wrong. If we didn't, we wouldn't try to hide it, either when we are doing it, or when we are confronted with the truth. Truth is God's way, and that is what He calls us to be, truth-tellers (Colossians 3:9). We never learn why Rachel took these household gods and it appears her deceit was never discovered, but God knew, and that is what should be our guide when considering either lying or deceiving (Numbers 32:23b). In the end, it is the truth that sets us free (John 8:31-21).

Lord, thank You for who You are, for Your goodness and mercy toward me, even when I am not always honest and, at times, am downright deceitful. I've even tested You – oh, how arrogant! – by praying about something I knew was wrong, but wanted You to condone it. Forgive me, Father, for ever having such a deceitful attitude. Search me, cleanse me, and continually change me so that I may be the child of God You intend for me to be. In the name of Jesus, I pray. Amen.

DAY 76

JACOB FLEES FROM LABAN
Read Genesis 31:20-55

By the time Laban caught up to Jacob's caravan, he was steaming, but he knew better than to say anything good or bad to Jacob because of God's admonition to him in a dream. And though he didn't do anything to Jacob or his caravan, Laban gave him a piece of his mind and let Jacob know the only reason he wasn't taking retribution was because God warned him not to (Genesis 31:20-24).

There was one matter that was heavily on Laban's mind, though. We can imagine his tone was somewhat indignant toward Jacob when he asked, "But why did you steal my gods?" Now it was Jacob's turn to be incensed. He had no idea what Laban was talking about and challenged him to search his entire camp to find what Laban was looking for, adding, "...if you find anyone who has your gods, that person shall not live."

Laban made an extensive search of all the tents, but when he came to Rachel's tent, she was sitting on the very place where she had hidden the household gods and said to her father, "Don't be angry, my lord, that I cannot stand up in your presence. I am having my period." She knew exactly how to continue her deceit because in those days, when women were having their period, it was often connected to impurity and, since impurity was contagious, the women were often isolated and untouchable.

Rachel's plan worked. Laban searched, but did not find the household gods, which made Jacob even more infuriated. He let loose on Laban like a bursting dam, pouring water out with enough force to destroy everything in its path. When confronted with what he knew was truth, Laban took a different approach to calm the waters by offering a solution to their problem, "Come now, let's make a covenant, you and I, and let it serve as a witness between us."

Do you see how when tempers are high, situations can escalate to a fever pitch? Jacob felt justified in leaving without telling Laban; Laban felt betrayed, and Rachel seemingly got away with her deception. God spoke to both of these men and so, when they finished venting, they began to think rationally about a solution to their problem.

Ephesians 4:25-27 says, "Therefore each of you must put off falsehood and speak truthfully to his neighbor for we are all members of one body. In your anger do not sin. Do not let the sun go down while you are still angry, and do not give the devil a foothold." Jacob and Laban were able to work through their difficulties, even having a meal together. Early the next morning Laban kissed his grandchildren and daughters and blessed them. Then he returned home (Genesis 31:54-55).

Anger, bitterness, resentment and self-justification result in even more anger, bitterness, resentment and self-justification. As Christ-followers, we must do nothing out of selfish ambition or vain conceit, but in humility consider others better than ourselves (Philippians 2:3). Then we can listen to what others are saying and ask the Lord in prayer for a resolution. In this way, all concerned can go away with a sense of peace, resulting in a blessing.

Lord, when I find myself in a heated argument, trying to make my point without listening to what the other person has to say, check me and help me to stop immediately. I know I am guilty of doing this very thing and so, I pray, that when this happens again, and it surely will, that You give me the presence of Your Spirit to listen, to pray and to seek Your help in finding a resolution that will bring peace and blessing to all involved. In the name of Jesus, I pray. Amen.

DAY 77

JACOB AT A CROSSROADS
Read Genesis 32:1-2

Jacob was at a crossroads in his life. He put his past behind him, but now he had to face an uncertain future. As his mind began to wander to his past, he remembered how much his brother Esau hated him, so much so that he even wanted to murder him. Jacob's heart was troubled. How could he continue on this journey into the unknown? This is when the angels of God met him, at his point of need. And when Jacob saw them, he said, "This is the camp of God!"

Like a volcano ready to burst forth, Jacob's excitement must have welled up within him knowing that God was with him on this journey. He could confidently take his family, as well as all his possessions, and begin in faith to move toward the place where God called him. It was such a memorable experience that Jacob named the place where the angels appeared to him, Mahanaim, meaning "two camps," the place where Jacob's past and future met (Genesis 32:1-2).

This is a good example of contemplation. The Lord did something extraordinary in Jacob's life, and Jacob took time to think about it. He was no longer a mama's boy who deceived and connived to get what he wanted. He had changed considerably since he left his family in Beersheba. Now he could continue his life in confidence because he knew that God was with him. He was so grateful that he took the time to thank God, setting up a place of remembrance.

Oftentimes I find myself in prayer asking God for things, not necessarily for myself, but for others. I have to admit that I become discouraged at times when I don't feel like there are any answers. However, when I delve into God's word and read how He hears our prayers (Psalm 34:17-19), how He cares for us (1 Peter 5:7), how He comforts us in all our troubles so that we can comfort those in trouble (2 Corinthians 1:3-4), I grow confident that He not only hears my prayers, but He will answer them if I put my complete trust in Him.

I've read stories of saints who have gone into glory, never knowing if their prayers were answered, but they trusted God to the very end. Like the story of George Mueller, whose legacy in Christ continues on to this very day. He struggled with knowing whether his brother and father found a relationship with Christ and went to heaven when they died. He went to the grave not knowing, but he knew God as just, so he put his trust in God, which allowed him to find peace.

So, like Jacob, let's look to the Lord God Almighty to help us forget what is behind, and strain toward what is ahead. May we press on toward the goal to win the prize for which God has called us heavenward in Christ Jesus (Philippians 3:13-14). This gives us confidence to trust God with our past and move forward towards our future, knowing that He hears our prayers and will answer them.

Lord, let me receive with gratitude the victories You give me. Help me to take time to sit with You, allowing You to minister to me in whatever form that might take. Help me to see where I have been, and how You have brought me through, so that I may go on my way in confidence that whatever lies ahead, You will make the way, and I have no reason to worry. In the precious name of Jesus, I pray. Amen.

DAY 78

JACOB PREPARES TO MEET ESAU
Read Genesis 32:3-21

Coming back to a family from whom you've been separated for 20 years is difficult, as Jacob was discovering when he considered what might be next in his journey home. I should know. As I mentioned earlier, I was separated from mine for over 30 years and the thought of reaching out for possible reconciliation was overwhelming. I didn't know where to begin, but I did begin. I prayed, sought God's help and guidance and put one step in front of the other. It resulted in a partial reconciliation. Family separations are not uncommon, but when we believe God and do what He tells us to do, there is always hope that things can change.

What must Jacob have been thinking as he gathered his family and belongings to continue this journey back home? Twenty years passed since he fled for his life and went to find safety among his mother's relatives. Yes, God told him to return to the land He promised Abraham and Isaac, and now him. The land that God said would eventually belong to their descendants. He must have had some misgivings, but he knew there was no turning back.

There was one big problem: His brother Esau lived there and they had had no contact during Jacob's absence. He didn't know if his parents were alive. He didn't know if Esau still harbored thoughts of murder against him for basically stealing the birthright, as well as the blessing from their father. Anyhow, He had a plan and he began to implement it by sending messengers ahead to find Esau and tell him, "Your servant Jacob says, 'I have been staying with Laban and have remained there till now'..." He was setting the stage to let Esau know he hadn't been hiding from him all this time and that, by referring to himself as a servant, he wasn't being proud or boastful. When the messengers returned and told Jacob that Esau was now coming to meet him with 400 men, that wasn't the answer he was hoping for, and great fear and distress came upon him (Genesis 32:3-7).

Times of fear should be times of prayer. Whatever frightens us should drive us to our knees and to our God, and that it did.[1] After implementing his plan and sending five separate herds of animals to meet Esau, instructing each of them to say to Esau, "...Jacob is coming behind us," he was left alone and had an encounter with God (Genesis 32:9-21).

It often takes courage and lots of faith to trust God when we're faced with daunting circumstances and decisions. James knew this when he wrote to the twelve tribes of Israel scattered among the nations, and he is telling us as well, "Consider it pure joy whenever you face trials of many kinds, because you know that the testing of your faith develops perseverance...Blessed is the man who perseveres under trial, because when he has stood the test, he will receive the crown of life that God has promised to those who love Him" (James 1:2-3, 12). Times of testing help us grow stronger when we look to the One who gives us strength.

Lord, what a hope I have in You when I trust You with the things I struggle with. May I never forget that You are my mighty tower, the One I can turn to in times of trouble. In the name of Jesus, I pray. Amen.

DAY 79

JACOB OVERCOMES AND IS BLESSED
Read Genesis 32:22-32

Jacob's father-in-law pursued him with ill intent, but because God intervened, they were able to work out their differences and part in peace. Jacob was venturing into the unknown, faced with an unavoidable, and perhaps deadly meeting with his brother Esau. Yet Jacob knew that God told him to go back to his homeland. This may have been the first time in a long time since he was alone with no distractions to steer him away from what God had for him. That night, after sending his wives, concubines, and 11 sons over the ford of the Jabbok River, he met a man, or so he thought at first, and wrestled with him until daybreak. Jacob was so intent on winning this struggle, he would not let go (Genesis 32:22-24).

I've done a vast amount of research about the meaning of this struggle. There are views running the gamut of it being a real physical struggle, or it possibly being a spiritual struggle. It's difficult to come to a firm conclusion, but it brings me to a question: Have you ever struggled with God, praying so intently that unless you received an answer, you were not going to let go? There have not been many of those times in my life, but the one I remember most I will share with you.

I have written several times about the separation from my family. Coming back and trying to mend relationships has been an emotional roller coaster that has not yet stopped to let its passengers disembark. Throughout this time, I lived in Florida and my family lived in California, but while my dad was still alive, I visited frequently.

One day I went for a walk and when I came back to the house I announced, "I'm back," but did not get an acknowledgement. I heard voices upstairs and began to listen. I didn't mean to eavesdrop, but I heard my name mentioned and the things I heard troubled me deeply. I walked back out of the house so hurt, ready to walk away once again in my distress. Instead, I walked to a park. I sat on a bench and prayed and prayed and prayed, refusing to leave until I received a word from the Lord, and I did. He said, "You are looking for affirmation in the wrong places. Look to Me."

There are no words to adequately describe the relief I felt when I heard this. I had been trying so hard to please everyone in the family, to get their approval and force them to love me, despite our differences. I had taken my focus away from the Lord and put it on them. The struggle was over, and I knew I could go back in peace.

I'm not certain this was the type of struggle Jacob was having, but does it really matter? He was determined to get relief from God and was not letting go. When the man saw he could not overpower Jacob, he touched the socket of Jacob's hip so that it was wrenched... But Jacob said, "I will not let go unless you bless me."

The man asked him, "What is your name?"

"Jacob," he answered.

"Your name will no longer be Jacob but Israel because you have struggled with God and with men and have overcome."

This was such a transformational event that God changed Jacob's name. He was no longer the man he used to be; He was a new person with a new name. Jacob was certainly rewarded for his tenaciousness. Then Jacob asked the man's name but he would not tell. So Jacob called the place "Peniel," because he saw God face to face and yet his life was spared (Genesis 32:25-30).

Jacob was touched by God and he was never the same. This is what happens when we discover Jesus, the Savior. When we give up our struggles with this world, He comes in and makes us a new creation in Him (2 Corinthians 5:17), and we are never the same.

Lord, may I come to the place where my struggles become blessings. In the process, help me to let go of the old and embrace the new, giving my heart, mind, soul and spirit to You to conform into the image of Jesus Christ, my Savior and King, in whose precious name, I pray. Amen.

DAY 80

JACOB AND ESAU MEET
Read Genesis 33:1-20

The lives of Esau and Jacob have all the makings for an intriguing movie: hatred, thoughts of murder, fleeing to another land, lying, deceit, polygamy, sibling rivalry, some, if not all, the things we deal with in today's world. What must have been going on in the minds of these twin brothers as they traveled towards each other?

Esau was traveling with 400 men, along the way encountering his brother's gifts. Was he prepared for battle, yet beginning to soften each time he heard Jacob's servants say to him, "... Jacob is coming behind us"? And Jacob, who just had an encounter with God, was he wavering in his trust and worrying about what Esau's intent toward him was? These are questions with untold answers. One thing was certain: They were about to meet.

When Jacob saw Esau coming with his 400 men, he divided his family into four segments and then went on ahead bowing to the ground seven times as he approached his brother. What was Esau's reaction? He threw his arms about Jacob's neck and kissed him. And they wept. Jacob's worries and fears had been for naught. What a relief to be held by his brother and kissed (Genesis 33:1-4).

In times of despair and worry, our thoughts should not be on how we can allay a situation but we should be in prayer, asking the Lord how we can submit to Him, allowing Him to work things through (Philippians 4:6). I can't tell you the countless hours I've spent through the years trying to manipulate others so that I could attain a certain outcome. I finally came to realize how wrong I've been. I now know this is not God's way. God is not a conniver or a deceiver. He doesn't do things underhandedly. He is always forthright and honest in his actions, which is what He wants us to be (1 Peter 1:13-16).

Before her sons were born, God told Rebekah the older would serve the younger (Genesis 25:23). Imagine how different things would have been if she had let God work this out instead of coming up with her own schemes, hurting not only her sons, but her husband. However, she didn't, and so we have this sad story of family disunity and distrust.

Fortunately for Esau and Jacob, they were able to show love to each other and reconcile, even though they didn't directly discuss the things that originally separated them. This may have been why Jacob did not want to go with Esau when he asked him to. Those too are details which are not written about, but the few details we have give me reason to think about how we might do better.

It's likely most of us have someone in our lives from whom we are separated because of harsh words, deceit or lying. It may be that one side or the other doesn't want to reconcile, but that doesn't mean we should stop praying for them. As long as there is breath, there is hope. Our responsibility is to trust God to do what He says He will do, and not go around Him by coming up with our own schemes and plans to get the results we desire.

Lord, help me to always be honest and forthright, not only with You, but everyone with whom I have dealings or interaction with. When I face situations that seem insurmountable, draw me to You by Your Holy Spirit so that I will stop to pray and seek Your guidance. I ask for patience to then wait upon You for an answer. In the name of Jesus, I pray. Amen.

DAY 81

JACOB'S SONS TAKE REVENGE
Read Genesis 34:1-31

*L*ife is full of bumps along the road. We never know when we might hit one so hard it will throw us off the road and take us down a path we hadn't anticipated. This is sometimes good, and sometimes bad. In Jacob's case, it was a really bad bump.

For 100 pieces of silver, Jacob bought a plot of ground from the sons of Hamor, the father of Shechem, and there he pitched his tent. He also set up an altar and called it El Elohe Israel, meaning "Mighty One" (Genesis 33:18-20).[1]

Jacob had a daughter named Dinah who ventured out to visit the women of the land. She met a man named Shechem and we are told that he violated her. We don't know if it was consensual or rape, but when Dinah's brothers found out about it, they were furious. Shechem (and his father) practically begged Jacob and Dinah's brothers to give her in marriage because he loved her. Dinah's brothers agreed, on one condition. Read very carefully because the words that came out of their mouths sounded as sweet as honey, but their hearts and minds were devising a deceitful plan of retribution (Genesis 34:1-17).

Our words. and those of others, have meaning, but they are not always truthful. I try very hard to not make a commitment I cannot keep, especially to children. But people do not always say what they mean or intend. Two of my friends are single mothers and I have seen the disappointment and hurt that the fathers of their children have caused by making promises and commitments that they never intended to keep. It hurts. We have all most likely been on the receiving end of something similar and it does something to us when this happens.

I don't know that we can ever with one-hundred percent certainty avoid hurting others or being hurt by others, but I do know with one-hundred percent certainty that we can trust our Heavenly Father because He always keeps His Word. He did it in the Old Testament, including foretelling what the future held. What was foretold took place in the New Testament, and the things foretold there will come to pass. So let's not get offended or too upset when friends and family let us down, but let's also be vigilant in prayer, especially when it appears something is too good to be true.

The Lord gave us these examples of human nature to show how this world operates at times. What we see and what we hear is not always the truth. Jesus told his disciples, "For false Christs and false prophets will appear and perform great signs and miracles to deceive even the elect, if that were possible. See I have told you this ahead of time" (Matthew 24:24-25). May we heed His warning and be vigilant.

What happened to Shechem and his father Hamor? They were delighted with the plans suggested by Dinah's brothers and agreed to them, as did their entire village. And while the men were still recovering and in pain, two of Jacob's sons, Simeon and Levi, Dinah's brothers, took their swords and attacked the unsuspecting city, killing every male. Then they took their sister

Dinah out of the house and left. To add insult to injury, the sons of Jacob looted the city, seized the flocks, herds and donkeys, and everything else in the city and out in the fields. They carried off all the wealth, along with the women and children, taking everything in the houses. This was a sad betrayal by God's people to do such a hideous thing. Jacob let them know how displeased he was with them, but they justified their actions and seemingly did not repent (Genesis 32:21-31).

As I've said several times throughout this devotional, honesty is always best, even when it hurts. Looking back on these tragic events, may we consider our own hearts when someone treats us unfairly, lies or steals from us. I know it's hard, but like Abraham, we can trust that God is the judge of all the earth and He will do what is right (Genesis 18:25). We don't have to be concerned with retribution.

Lord, thank You once again for not sugarcoating the actions of Your people in the Old Testament. What Jacob's sons did was deceitful and wrong, but let me not be their judge, for I know I too have been deceitful and wrong. I don't know what Your judgment was on them, but I can be certain You did what was right and just. Help me do right, but when I have done wrong, help me to acknowledge it quickly, ask forgiveness and do all I can to make things right. In the name of Jesus, I pray. Amen.

DAY 82

JACOB RETURNS TO BETHEL
Read Genesis 35:1-15

Jacob, like his grandfather Abraham, seemed to have a difficult time staying focused on God's direction for his life. He'd had an encounter with God when he left his father-in-law Laban and began his return to the Promised Land. On his way, he got distracted and ended up in a place where God did not intend him to be.

Sound familiar? I've been there, more than once. The human will is strong. Our culture leads us to believe we have it within ourselves to be whatever it is we want to be, that there are no limits to what we can do if we just try hard enough, fight long enough or work harder. That attitude often sets us up for failure, disappointment and discouragement. Why? Because we are designed to be who and what God created us to be, not who or what we think we can be on our own.

Each one of us is unique and we have purpose; our lives have meaning. If we could only understand we are not here for our own purposes, but for His purpose, life would make much more sense.

Habits and thoughts that are ingrained in us from childhood are hard to break. Jacob, like most of us, was finding that out. If he'd heard God speak, perhaps the incident with Dinah and the subsequent massacre would never have happened. We can't go there, though, because it did happen and there were serious consequences. In this, God got Jacob's attention and told him to go back to Bethel, the place where he first met God as he fled his brother Esau more than twenty years earlier. It was there that God affirmed Jacob's name change to "Israel" and restated to him the promise He gave to Abraham and Isaac of an inheritance of the land to their descendants (Genesis 35:1-10).

Because of God's faithfulness in keeping His covenant, His plan was fulfilled, through imperfect people. When we turn to the book of Matthew and read the genealogy of Jesus, we find a murderer, liars, cheaters, a gentile, a prostitute, and many more ancestors with other faults, until we come to Jesus who, though He was without sin, is able to empathize with our weaknesses. He was tempted in every way just as we are (Hebrews 4:15). And because of Christ's faithfulness, the Spirit of God testifies with our spirit that we are God's children.

Now, if we are children, then we are heirs, heirs of God and co-heirs with Christ, if indeed we share in His sufferings in order that we may also share in His glory (Romans 8:16-17). This is who we are. When we believe in Jesus Christ, we become children of God, brothers and sisters of Christ, and we are gifted with the inheritance which belongs to Him, who not only died on the cross for our sins, but was resurrected from the dead and now sits at the right hand of God (Colossians 3:1). That is an inheritance worth waiting for.

Lord, thank You that because of Jesus, I have become Your child. What a day that will be when You call me into Your kingdom to live in eternity with You. Thank You for Your promises that never fail. In the name of Jesus, I pray. Amen.

DAY 83

THE DEATHS OF RACHEL AND ISAAC
Read Genesis 35:16-29

*I*f Jacob thought life was going to be a piece of cake after he returned wholeheartedly to God, he's about to discover it will be anything but that. Soon thereafter, Rachel died in childbirth. Before her death, she named her son Ben-Oni, meaning, "son of my sorrow." Perhaps Jacob didn't want his son to feel responsible for his mother's death as he got older, or be reminded that Rachel died while giving birth to him, so Jacob renamed their son Benjamin, which means, "very dear to me," or "set on my right hand as a blessing" (Genesis 35:16-20).

Adding insult to injury, Reuben, Jacob's firstborn and the son of Leah, desired to immediately claim leadership over the entire clan. To do this, he slept with Jacob's concubine Bilhah, something which would not only have disgraced her in the eyes of the rest of the family, but would be like claiming your inheritance before the actual death of the father. The custom of taking a father's concubines was reserved for after a father died. It was much more than a sexual act. It was claiming a position of leadership and authority. We are told Israel (Jacob) heard about what his son did, but it already happened and nothing could change that (Genesis 35:22).

Customs were far different back then, but the turmoil, struggle and pain is the same today, even if the circumstances are different. And just because Jacob's life changed, and he was fully committed to God, it didn't mean everything would be easy. When I first became a Christian, I used to wonder if life would now be boring and uneventful, and if there would be challenges, good or bad. I'd just sit back, read the Bible, talk to God and wait for Jesus to come back. I was not prepared for my rude awakening.

As Christians, we can't expect life to be free from heartache (Luke 9:23; 2 Timothy 3:12). When we read about the lives of the prophets, judges, kings and others in the Old Testament, their lives were extremely difficult. The same is true for the New Testament. John is the only apostle who died a natural death. All the rest were martyred.

At the end of this chapter, Isaac died at one-hundred and eighty years old and was buried by his sons, Esau and Jacob. Isaac lived much longer than he thought he would. Fortunately, for these men, it meant reconciliation, not only for Jacob and father, but for Esau and Jacob. This might be a good time to consider our own family estrangements and think about reconciliation before it's too late. It's not always possible, but a simple phone call or visit might bring unexpected results. We won't know unless we put ourselves out there and try.

The twelve sons of Jacob are listed in a genealogy before the account of Isaac's death. This is significant in that it tells us Jacob (renamed Israel) is now the patriarch of the covenant made with Abraham and Isaac, and it is through him, and the lineage of one of his sons, that the Messiah will one day come.

Lord, sometimes life with Jesus seems harder than life without Him when I don't understand the pain and suffering I am experiencing. Help me, as Your child, to know that this world is full of pain and suffering and it will always be this way until the end of time. May I receive Your grace and mercy during my trying times, and realize that my life is meant to give glory and honor to You, even when I suffer. Until the day You take me home, or until Jesus returns, may I never forget that You will never leave nor forsake me all the days of my life. In the name of Jesus, I pray. Amen.

DAY 84

ESAU'S DESCENDANTS
Read Genesis 36

Sometimes I come to a chapter or verse in the Bible and wonder, "Why is this included? Is it really necessary to know this?" That is my question for Chapter 36, which is a long list of people that none of us know, except for the one about whom the chapter is written: Esau, whom God told his mother Rebekah would become one of two nations.

Why do we need to read about his descendants, most of whose names we cannot pronounce and won't remember by the time we finish reading them? Well, the Bible is much more than something to read. It is full of real-life people who tell God's story in a way that reveals who we are.

You might ask, what does that mean? If you haven't noticed by now, there is a consistent theme taking place between those who serve God and those who do not, like Cain and Abel, Ishmael and Isaac, and now, Esau and Jacob.

Esau was a man of the world. Despite his careless behavior in forfeiting his birthright for a cup of stew and losing his father's blessing, he prospered. One thing was lacking though. There is no mention that he served the One True God or even knew about Him.

As God's story continues throughout the Old Testament, we will encounter Esau's descendants, who became known as Edomites. In the book of Exodus we will read that when the Israelite people requested permission to pass through their land, they refused them, and from that time forward, they were hostile toward Israel, the descendants of Abraham, Isaac and Jacob (Numbers 20:14-21).

The website *Compelling Truth* puts it this way:

> Between the Old and New Testament times, the Edomites were once again controlled by the Jews and forced to embrace Judaism. In the Greek language, that gained prominence during this time, their name became the Idumaeans. King Herod was an Idumaean and ruled at the time of the birth of Jesus; he also commanded the deaths of all males two years old and under in Bethlehem in order to kill the threat of a Jewish king (Matthew 2:16-18).
>
> The Edomites, by then known as the Idumaeans, eventually disappear from history. One of the last mentions of the Idumeans was a reference to the land of Idumea by the church leader Jerome around AD 400. The prediction that Esau (the Edomites) would serve Jacob (the Israelites) proved true.[1]

This is one more example of God's word coming to pass, helping to build the foundation upon which our faith is based.

Lord, keep me focused on what Your purpose is in everything written in Your word. I may not remember it all, or even understand it, but thank You that I can count on the truth of it. In the name of Jesus, I pray. Amen.

DAY 85

THE TWELVE SONS
Read Genesis 37:1-11

*J*acob had twelve sons (from four different women), but Judah, son number four, is the lineage from which Jesus comes. The most prominent figure throughout the rest of Genesis is Jacob's eleventh son, Joseph, known as "the dreamer" by his brothers. Joseph was the son of Rachel, whom Jacob loved, and was highly favored, which led to jealousy amongst his older brothers.

I love the story of Joseph because it is the Old Testament mirror image of Jesus in the New. He was faithful to God, with no record of sinning. We will learn that he was God's chosen one to save His people during a time of great famine.

When Joseph was seventeen, he had dreams. He shared those dreams with his father and brothers. They rebuked him, thinking he was trying to make something of himself that he shouldn't. One of the dreams involved binding up sheaves of grain out in the field when, suddenly, Joseph's sheaf rose and stood upright, while the other sheaves gathered around and bowed down to it. The brothers ridiculed Joseph saying, "Do you intend to reign over and rule us?" Little did they know, that was exactly what would take place (Genesis 37:1-11).

One thing I've learned from this story is how to trust the Lord in all circumstances of our lives. When everything seems to be going in the wrong direction, and life seems hopeless and lonely, don't lose faith in the Lord because He is faithful (Deuteronomy 7:9; Hebrews 10:23).

At times we are tried and tested. The way we respond makes a difference in the final outcome. Had Joseph not been faithful throughout all of his trials, God's plan would have come to pass in some other way, but it's encouraging to see that with God's strength and help we, like Joseph, can become overcomers.

Thank you, Father, for Your faithfulness. I ask today to receive a measure of faith from You and may that faith continue to grow within me as I read Your word and pray. Give me strength and hope to endure the trials of life, knowing that Your faithfulness will bring me through. In the name of Jesus, I pray. Amen.

DAY 86

SOLD INTO SLAVERY
Read Genesis 37:12-36

When Joseph's brothers were grazing the flocks in the fields, Jacob sent Joseph to see if all was well with them, and to report back to him. When Joseph's brothers saw him coming they conspired to kill him. They threw him into a cistern and took off the richly ornamented robe which his father made him. Later, Reuben, the oldest brother, had a change of heart and went back to retrieve Joseph from the cistern, but it was too late. He was sold to a passing caravan, who later sold him in Egypt to Potiphar, one of Pharaoh's officials (Genesis 37:12-30).

Joseph's brothers killed a goat, dipped the robe in its blood and took it back to their father saying, "We found this. Examine it to see whether it is your son's robe." When Jacob recognized the robe, he said, "It is my son's robe. Some ferocious animal has devoured him." Jacob was left to believe that his son had been eaten by a wild animal and his other sons didn't tell him otherwise (Genesis 37:31-36).

There is a lot going on in this family of God. Which one are you? Are you the jealous one? Or maybe you're the favorite? Maybe you are an only child who thinks the world is yours because you are constantly the center of attention? Or maybe singleness causes resentment against your parents for not having more children? Are you a parent who has lost a child?

No matter our situation, we all have feelings about who we are in the family and what we consider our rightful place to be. Because we are all human, most of us are never satisfied. The only true satisfaction comes when we turn our eyes to the One who chose when we were born, and to whom we were born. Joseph knew this, and it gave him confidence – perhaps too much at times – to know that no matter his circumstances, God was with him.

God is looking for those who will trust Him - no matter their position in the family, no matter their position at work and no matter their financial situation. He wants to know, "Will you trust Me every day, no matter the struggles?" Joseph, like all of us, had more than his fair share of troubles. He was taken away from his family and sold into slavery. He was falsely accused of wrongdoing. He was forgotten and forsaken in a dingy prison, but he never once blamed God; he never wavered in his faith. As Christians, we should be like Joseph and do the same.

Lord, may my heart be filled with the knowledge of who You are, that You are faithful, You are loving, You are kind and You never forsake Your children in their time of adversity. Help me to trust You more each day so that when the difficulties come, I look to You for my source of strength. In the name of Jesus, I pray. Amen.

DAY 87

JUDAH AND TAMAR
Read Genesis 38:1-24

Judah is the fourth son of Jacob and Leah. He is also an ancestor in the lineage of Jesus Christ. When we read about the events in Chapter 38, be prepared for a mind-blowing event that helps us discover the imperfection of God's people, and in the process come to realize our own imperfections.

For whatever reason, Judah left his family and went to stay with a man named Hirah, who was a Canaanite. The Canaanites, as we will learn later, occupied the land that would one day belong to the descendants of Abraham, Isaac and Jacob. They were not believers in the One True God of Israel, and it seems that Hirah had quite an influence on Judah in forsaking the One True God, for he married a Canaanite woman. They had three sons (Genesis 38:1-5).

This might be a good time to consider who we hang out with and the influences they have on our lives. It's not that there's anything wrong with having friends who don't believe what we do about Jesus, but if that's who we spend most of our time with, they will undoubtedly have an influence on us. They will most likely lead us away from our first love - Jesus. If He is not first in our friends' lives, most likely, He won't be in ours either.

When Er, Judah's oldest son, was of marrying age, Judah chose a Canaanite woman for him named Tamar. Er was wicked in the Lord's sight, so He put him to death (Genesis 38:7). It was customary in those days, if a married son died without children and there were other sons in the family, that the next in line would take the dead son's place and marry his widow. There are different opinions on why this was done, but they pretty much boil down to the issue of giving the deceased son's inheritance to a rightful heir.

By keeping the widow in the family, she could become pregnant by the dead son's brother, thereby preserving his inheritance so the family could be provided for. That also meant the son marrying the widow would no longer have an eldest son for his own inheritance. So when Judah gave his second son Onan to Tamar, Onan didn't want her to get pregnant. Whenever they had intercourse, he would spill his semen on the ground so she wouldn't become pregnant. This also was wicked in the Lord's sight, so He put Onan to death (Genesis 38:8-10).

Imagine Judah's misery at losing two of his three sons. He'd given both of them to the same woman to marry, and they both died. Understandably, he might have some apprehension about giving his remaining son to Tamar.

Judah then sent Tamar to live with her father, which was highly unusual, as her father had no legal obligation to let her come back home. Time passed. When Shelah was old enough to marry Tamar, she heard nothing. We don't know how long she waited, but it was long enough for her to know she was being ignored by her father-in-law. She decided to take matters into her own hand (Genesis 38:11).

After Judah's wife died, and he recovered from his grief, he went with his friend Hirah to a shearing of the sheep in another town named Timnah. Tamar learned about this and quickly removed her widow's clothes. She found a place on the road to Timnah, covered her face with a veil, and waited. Women in those days had no means to provide for themselves. If their husband died and left no heir, they were relegated to a life of poverty. Tamar obviously wasn't the type of woman to take that sitting down. She wanted to get pregnant one way or another, even if it meant deception. Maybe she was hopeful Shelah, Judah's youngest son, would be with his father, but when she didn't see him, she was satisfied with tricking her father-in-law, who liked what he saw on his way to Timnah (Genesis 38:12-14).

Unlike his father, Judah had one wife and didn't remarry. When he saw what was "pleasing to the eye" (remember Eve?), he wanted it. He and Tamar had their tryst and Tamar got what she went for, procuring Judah's seal, cord, and staff as collateral for the goat he promised to bring her the next day. When Judah sent his friend back with the goat the next day to retrieve his items, the townspeople denied the existence of a prostitute on the road to Timnah. When he told Judah, he dropped the matter. Even though he'd lost the items that identified him, he didn't want to pursue it further lest he becomes a laughing stock among the people. What others might think influenced him more than procuring what was rightfully his (Genesis 38:15-23).

How often have we let what others think about us influence our decisions, especially when it comes to our relationship with Jesus? To be honest, I've been intimidated by those who think my beliefs are whacky. I often shy away from confrontation for fear of making someone else feel their opinion doesn't matter, even if I know what they are saying is wrong. I've found myself, many times through the years, apologizing to the Lord in prayer for not being more confident in who I am in Him and what He has done for me through the saving power and grace of Jesus Christ.

I know what He did to change my life and I want everyone I

love to have that same experience, but I often sit quietly when they ridicule my faith or use arguments to counter what I believe. I don't like to admit this because after forty-plus years I should know how to express what I believe. Instead, I live my life in a way that manifests His presence, praying that my actions speak louder than my words.

Lord, thank You for letting me know how imperfect Your people in the Old Testament were and, as I am about to learn, how faithful You were in redeeming them. I'm feeling super blessed to be living at this point in time, with the knowledge of who Jesus is and why He came to die for my sins. I'm also thankful that He not only died, but He rose from the dead and is coming back one day to set up His kingdom. You've written it all down in this one book that I can read over and over again, leaving no doubt as to how I got here, why I am here, and where I am going when I die. May my days be filled with showing others what it means to be a child of God Almighty, the Creator of heaven and earth. Amen.

DAY 88

TRUTH AND CONSEQUENCES
Read Genesis 38:24-30

Tamar had tenacity. She was a woman with a strong will who knew what she wanted and what she felt she deserved. Not only did she disguise herself as a prostitute and then have sex with her father-in-law, she got pregnant. About three months later she was unable to keep it a secret, but was prepared for a confrontation. When Judah was told about her condition, he commanded, "Bring her out and have her burned to death!" (Genesis 38:24).

We must be careful what we say, or it may come back to bite us the moment the words leave our lips. It did with Judah, for when Tamar was brought out to her father-in-law she sent a message to let him know who the father of her children was. When he saw his seal, cord, and staff, there was no denying it. What he desired most, not to be laughed at by others, was magnified even greater now that his secret was known to his entire world. He did not try and deny it, but said, "She is more righteous than me, since I wouldn't give her to my son Shelah" (Genesis 38:25-26).

Tamar was pregnant with twins. There is not much said about the birth except that the one whose wrist was tied with a scarlet thread when he stuck his hand out first, was actually born second. It's a parallel to Esau and Jacob, except their birthrights were exchanged after they were born, much later in life. Here we have Perez, meaning "breaking out," and Zerah meaning "scarlet" or "brightness."[1] Zerah was the first to announce he was coming out, but Perez broke out in front and got the title (Genesis 38:27-30).

This is a story of self-will to get what you want because you believe with all your heart you're entitled to it, and you do get what you want. Notice that there is no mention of the Lord in all of this. It is entirely the determination of the person to get what they want, whether it's good for them or not. Then there is Judah who knew he was wrong in not giving his son to Tamar, but figured he could get away with it without consequence. He was contrite when his sin was discovered and seems to have made peace with the Lord about it.

Turning to Matthew, the first book in the New Testament, the first chapter, we read the genealogy of Jesus Christ. Who do we find mentioned in the lineage? Not only Judah and Perez, but Tamar; one of only three women mentioned. Tamar was a Canaanite, who did not serve the Living God; Ruth was a Gentile, who came from a culture of idol worship, and Rahab was a prostitute.

These were people just like you and me. We're not prostitutes or idol worshipers, but we are all sinners. Isn't this an amazing story of redemption by our Loving Heavenly Father, who said His Son was coming to earth to set men free and He was prepared to use whoever He could to get the job done.

He loves us so much, with all of our faults. He doesn't turn away from us or leave us when we do wrong. He continually calls out to us, "Return to me and I will return you" (Zechariah 1:3

and Malachi 3:7). If we confess our sins, God is faithful and just and will forgive us our sins, and purify us from all unrighteousness (1 John 1:9). He did it for those in the Old Testament and He did it for us in the New. All we are told to do is believe (Romans 10:9).

Lord, thank You so much for giving the message in Your word that You want me to come before You in my fallen condition, because this is the only way I can come to You. You give me explicit, detailed instructions on how I can come out of that condition, by asking Jesus to forgive my sins. You also promise that if I continue in my faith, I am without blemish and free from accusation (Colossians 1:22-23). What a mighty loving God You are. Amen.

DAY 89

POTIPHAR'S WIFE
Read Genesis 39:1-23

Joseph's brothers stripped him of his coat and stained it with goat's blood in order to trick their father into believing he was dead, but they couldn't strip Joseph of his virtue and faith. They separated Joseph from his father's house, but they couldn't separate Joseph from his God.[1]

When he arrived in Egypt, those who took him from the cistern sold him to Potiphar, an Egyptian who was one of Pharaoh's officials and captain of the guard. Joseph was only seventeen, maybe eighteen, at the time, but there is no indication he was ever fearful or full of self-pity while all of this was taking place. He apparently did what Potiphar commanded him to do (Colossians 3:22-25). It didn't take long for Potiphar to realize Joseph was blessed by God. He soon put Joseph in charge of his entire household and did not concern himself with anything except the food he ate (Genesis 39:1-6).

What a statement of God's favor. By not complaining, being obedient and willing to take each day and live it to its fullest, Joseph, though a slave, was rewarded mightily. He went about his duties in Potiphar's house until one day Potiphar's wife laid eyes on him and desired to have sex with him. He refused, saying, "How could I do such a wicked thing and sin against God?" (Genesis 39:7-9).

Scripture tells us to flee temptation, to not even let its desire take hold of us in our hearts (1 Corinthians 6:18; 10:13, Matthew 5:27-28). Joseph knew this and he refused to even be around Potiphar's wife until one day when none of the household servants were inside, she caught Joseph by his cloak and said, "Come to bed with me!" He left his cloak in her hand and fled out of the house (Genesis 39:10-12).

Hell has no fury like a woman scorned.[2] She wasn't going to be made a laughing stock. Once she realized she could use Joseph's cloak as evidence, she accused him of accosting her and making a fool of her and Potiphar.[3]

Have you ever been wrongly accused? Most of us can probably think of a time or two. If or when this happens, we shouldn't seek or desire revenge; it will consume us. The Lord will fight for us; we need only be still (Exodus 14:14). Also, we are told to "consider it pure joy, my brothers, whenever you face trials of many kinds, because you know that the testing of your faith develops perseverance" (James 1:2). We are not to "repay anyone evil for evil. But be careful to do what is right in the eyes of everybody…Do not take revenge but leave room for God's wrath, for it is written, 'It is mine to avenge; I will repay,' says the Lord" (Romans 12:17, 19).

What must Potiphar have thought when he heard his wife's story? He knew how faithful Joseph had been and how he himself was blessed because of Joseph. As captain of the guard to Pharaoh, he had a very high position and could have easily ordered Joseph's execution due to his wife's accusation.

It seems he may have been doubtful as to his wife's account

of things because Potiphar instead sent Joseph to prison, the place normally reserved for those awaiting trial, judgment or execution. It wasn't long until Joseph's faithfulness to God was rewarded in prison, for the warden put Joseph in charge of all those held in prison. He also was made responsible for all that was done there. The Lord gave Joseph success in whatever he did.

This account of Joseph's life is just beginning. Every time I read his story it gives me encouragement to know that when things are going awry, nothing is going my way, God is still there. I am reminded that God is always faithful (2 Timothy 2:13) and that in all things God works for the good of those who love Him, who have been called according to His purpose (Romans 8:28). Let's not allow discouragement or depression take hold of us when we know we have been wronged. Let's look to our Heavenly Father, knowing that He sees our dilemma and He will not forsake us in our time of need. Sometimes it takes a while so we must be patient.

Lord, thank You again for the life of Joseph with all he endured, being sold into slavery, wrongly accused and forgotten. May his example encourage me to always look to You in my difficult times, in my worries, in my heartache and in my pain. I ask for Your patience and endurance, especially during these times, trusting that You see, hear and answer in Your perfect time. In the name of Jesus, I pray. Amen.

DAY 90

JOSEPH INTERPRETS DREAMS
Read Genesis 40

*P*haraoh's cupbearer and baker for some unstated reason were put into prison. It's interesting that the prison was in the house of the captain of the guard (Genesis 40:1-3). Do you remember who that was? It was Potiphar, who assigned Joseph to attend to these two men.

They'd been there for quite some time when Joseph noticed one day that the two men were sad. He asked them, "Why the sadness?" Both had dreams and they were feeling dejected because there was no one to interpret them. Joseph said to them, "Do not interpretations belong to God? Tell me your dreams," and they did. After the cupbearer finished, Joseph interpreted his dream. Then the baker told Joseph his dream. It wasn't such a good outcome, but Joseph still interpreted it for him (Genesis 40:4-19).

As a Christian, I am often inclined to tell others only the goodness of God, but there is another side to Him. He is also a just God and will one day judge the living and the dead (1 Peter 4:5, Colossians 3:25). Jesus tells us, "I am the way, the truth and the life. No one comes to the Father except through me" (John 14:6). Yes, God is good, but there is only one way to approach Him in order to discover His goodness.

Our faith in Jesus Christ is not some made-up whim of man that comes and goes with the wind. It is faith in a real person, who lived a real life, who was the real Son of God, who came to earth to die for our sins, who rose from the dead, and who told us, "Behold, I am coming soon! My reward is with me, and I will give to everyone according to what he has done" (Revelation 22:12).

There is no escaping His judgment. If you don't believe in Him now while on this earth, you will when the *Book of Life* is open and your name is nowhere to be found. At that moment, it will be too late. If anyone's name is not found written in the *Book of Life*, he will be thrown into the lake of fire (Revelation 20:15).

Three days later, the baker was hanged, just as Joseph told him would happen; the cupbearer was restored to Pharaoh's palace, just as Joseph told him. Joseph knew he was wrongly imprisoned and said to the cupbearer after the interpretation of his dream, "When all goes well with you, remember me and show me kindness. Mention me to Pharaoh and get me out of this prison." However, when the chief cupbearer was restored to the palace, he did not remember Joseph; he forgot him (Genesis 40:20-23).

Matthew Cook, a pastor from Centerpoint Baptist Church, ended his sermon on Joseph with these words,

> "Joseph's fellow sufferers were like the two thieves that were crucified with Christ. One was saved, but the other condemned. The one that was saved, however, forgot about Joseph and his plea in Genesis 40:14. Contrast that with Christ. When the dying thief asked to be remembered, Christ was faithful to do so in saying, 'Today you will be with Me in

paradise!' Even though Joseph was forgotten by a man, he would never be forgotten by God."[1]

And God will never forget us, either (Psalm 27:10, Isaiah 49:15).

Thank You, Lord, that You are not only loving and kind but that You are also just. May I live my life each day as unto You and may I be pleasing in Your sight. And on that day when I take my last breath, may I enter Your presence for all eternity (John 17:2-3). In the name of Jesus, I pray. Amen.

DAY 91

PHARAOH AND HIS DREAM
Read Genesis 41:1-40

Joseph was enslaved and imprisoned for over twelve years, but his life was about to change drastically. Two full years after the cupbearer was restored to his position in the palace, he remembered Joseph. It wasn't something that happened out of the blue. It was only after Pharaoh had two dreams that troubled him greatly, but his magicians and wise men were unable to interpret them. Then the cupbearer said to Pharaoh, "A while back you imprisoned both me and the chief baker. We both had dreams. A young Hebrew who was in prison with us interpreted them and they came to pass exactly as he said." Pharaoh wasted no time in sending for Joseph, who was taken quickly from the dungeon, cleaned up and brought before Pharaoh (Genesis 41:1-14).

I get excited about what took place in this story. Here is Joseph, perhaps many times wondering, "When will God ever deliver me from these dingy, dark walls. I have done nothing to deserve this; yet here I am." Then, in one moment, he goes from prison to palace. He may not have realized at first what was taking place, but he would soon find out his patience, faithfulness, and prayers were being answered, in God's perfect timing.

Pharaoh said to Joseph, "I had a dream and no one can interpret it. But I have heard it said of you that when you hear a dream, you can interpret it." Joseph quickly responded, "I cannot do it, but God will give Pharaoh the answer he desires." Pharaoh told Joseph his dreams and God gave Joseph the interpretation. Then Joseph made suggestions about how to prepare for the seven-year famine that would take place after seven years of plenty. Finding no one more qualified to be in a position to implement this plan, Pharaoh appointed Joseph in charge of his palace and said, "All my people are to submit to your orders. Only with respect to the throne will I be greater than you."

Imagine how Joseph must have felt at his good fortune. Finally, after all these years of slavery and imprisonment, he was not only free, but given a position of authority over all of Pharaoh's people. He never lost sight of God in all of this. He remained faithful, humble, loyal and trustworthy, for he also knew that God had a plan and all of his misfortune was a part of it.

Have there ever been times in your life where you thought, "things can't get any worse," and then they do? Have you ever gotten frustrated with God, even mad at him, or felt abandoned by Him? If so, read about Joseph as many times as it takes to sink in that if anyone had reason to feel this way about God, Joseph did. Not once did he blame God for anything that was happening to him. Not once did he take credit for being able to interpret dreams. Not once did he become resentful or prideful. By his actions, it's evident that he always trusted God no matter what was happening to him.

Each event in the Bible has meaning and purpose. It's not only the history of God's people but it is our history as well. God never forces us to serve Him. He gives us a choice, and when we choose Him, He will use us for His purposes on earth. Joseph had no idea this was going to happen to him, but when it did, he was prepared for it because of all he went through. If we trust God when we are going through things we do not understand, He will do the same for us. It may not be second in command to Pharaoh, but it will be for His glory.

Lord, I am blessed to have Your written word that tells us the whole story. I don't have to wonder what is going to happen because I already know. My struggle comes when things happen to me that I don't understand because I don't see the whole picture. Give me a measure of faith to trust that You know what You are doing and everything will work out according to Your will. In the name of Jesus, I pray. Amen.

DAY 92

FROM SERVANT TO RULER
Read Genesis 41:41-52

*T*hroughout the land of Egypt, there was no one more powerful than Joseph. Pharaoh not only clothed him in robes of fine linen and put a gold chain around his neck, he took his signet ring and put it on Joseph's finger. At that time the signet ring of Pharaoh meant that any edict, order, document or other elements of society sealed with his ring had preeminence.

How must Joseph have felt when all this happened? He didn't sit around and become egotistical, taking advantage of his new position. He went right to work, traveling throughout Egypt. For the next seven years, he collected all the food produced in Egypt and stored up huge quantities of grain, like the sand of the sea, in each of the cities he visited (Genesis 41:41-49).

Joseph took his calling seriously. He believed the dreams God showed Pharaoh would happen and he went about doing God's work so as to be prepared when the famine came. I don't know when you are reading this or at what stage of life you are in, but right now our nation and the world are going through a crisis like we never thought possible. Our businesses are shut down. Our church doors are locked. Most states have issued a "stay-at-home" order, all because of an unseen virus that is indiscriminately ravaging the lives of many.

I don't know if the Lord spoke to any of His people about this before it happened, but I believe, for those who are living through it this very day (April 5th, 2020, Palm Sunday), it would serve us well to be on our knees in prayer, seeking the Lord with all of our hearts so that we are prepared when our day to leave this earth comes. This is what all the fear and anxiety is about. People are afraid to die. However, God told us how to prepare for its inevitability. If we, like Joseph, listen to Him, we will be prepared when that day comes, for Jesus has given us power over death, hell and the grave. His victory makes us victorious (1 Corinthians 15:55-57).

Before the famine came, Pharaoh gave Joseph the Egyptian name Zaphenath-Paneah (Genesis 41:45). Though there is no consensus as to its meaning, one source says it may mean, "revealer of secrets."[1] Whatever its meaning, it allowed Joseph to be more easily integrated into Egyptian society. Pharaoh also gave Joseph a wife named Asenath, daughter of Potiphera, priest of On. They had two sons. Joseph named the firstborn Manasseh, meaning God made it possible for him to forget his trouble; and the second son he named Ephraim, meaning fruitful (Genesis 41:50-52). There is no question God brought Joseph out of his troubles and made him fruitful.

Many times throughout biblical history God changes a person's name: Abram to Abraham, Jacob to Israel, Saul to Paul. Its significance is that the old has passed away and now a new time has begun. Jesus explained this to Nicodemus when He said, "You must be born again." Jesus did not mean born again by natural birth, but to be born of the spirit (John 3:5-21).

Before this new birth happens, we are alienated from God and enemies in our minds because of our evil behavior. Still, God reconciles us by Christ's physical body through death to present us holy in His sight, without blemish and free from accusation, if we continue in our faith" (Colossians 1:21-23).

Joseph's name was changed by Pharaoh in order to give him a new identity as an Egyptian noble.[2] Jesus said, "To him who overcomes... I will also give him a white stone with a new name written on it, known only to him who receives it" (Revelation 2:17). We don't know yet what heaven will be like but He who is seated on the throne said, "I am making everything new! Write this down, for these words are trustworthy and true" (Revelation 21:5). Unlike the Egyptian kingdom which through the centuries became powerless, the kingdom of Jesus Christ will never end (Luke 1:33).

Lord, thank You for Joseph's obedience to prepare for the day of famine so that his family, Your chosen people, would be saved. Thank You also for sending Your Son Jesus to save me from my sins. You are not willing that any should be lost but that all should come to repentance (2 Peter 2:9). You know the plans You have for me, and for that I am thankful. Help me to always be in an attitude of prayer so that I am prepared for whatever may befall me, even death. In the name of Jesus, I pray. Amen.

DAY 93

THE BROTHERS TRAVEL TO EGYPT
Read Genesis 41:53-57 & 42

By the time the seven years of famine began, Joseph was close to 40 years old. He'd been second in command to Pharaoh for over seven years, gathering so much grain in all the cities of Egypt it could not even be counted. When the people cried out to Pharaoh for food, he told them, "Go to Joseph and do what he tells you." Joseph was prepared and began opening up the storehouses to sell grain to the Egyptians (Genesis 41:53-57).

Sometimes I wonder if at this point Joseph was aware of his calling and purpose for being in the position the Lord put him. There's no indication he wavered in his faith or took advantage of others. He was going about the Lord's work, preparing for what he knew was coming. Are we prepared, like Joseph, for whatever the Lord may have in store for us?

No, we are not all Josephs, and we won't all be second in command to a world leader, but God does have a plan for us.

When we go through trials and difficult times, it is then we need to seek Him diligently, drawing so close to Him that trust is never an issue. Like Joseph, the difficulties may be the times we need to go through to prepare us for what is ahead.

For Joseph, the pieces of the puzzle were coming together when his brothers arrived on the scene. They had no idea who he was. They just knew they needed grain and he was the one in charge. He spoke quite harshly to them, even accused them of being spies to see where Egypt was unprotected. They denied any wrong intentions, but Joseph put them all in jail for three days anyway (Genesis 42:1-17).

What must the brothers have been thinking during this time? Were they contrite? Were they scared and worried about what was going to happen to them? They had no idea the man whom they had bowed down to was their brother, but Joseph knew them and he remembered his earlier dream as a young boy that they would one day bow down to him.

What was Joseph thinking? Was he seeking the Lord's help and guidance about what to do? Was he coming to realize that this was why he went through those tough times, so he could be in a position to help his family in their time of need? There is not much doubt they were pretty concerned and worried about their futures and whether they were even going to survive. After three days in prison, Joseph ordered his brothers to be brought before him. He said to them, "...I fear God. So here is the deal: You can go back home with the grain but one of your brothers has to stay behind." He chose Simeon and bound him before their very eyes (Genesis 42:18-19).

Joseph said further, "When you return for more grain, bring your youngest brother with you so that you may not die." They knew this request would be met with resistance from their father but they had no choice. As they discussed their situation among themselves, they said, "Surely we are being punished because of our brother (Joseph). We saw how distressed he was when he pleaded with us for his life, but we would not listen;

that's why this distress has come upon us." Joseph wept when he heard this. It must have been difficult for him to keep his identity hidden, but he longed to see his younger brother. As long as his identity was kept from them, they were sure to return with Benjamin if they wanted more grain (Genesis 42:20-24).

It's doubtful Joseph was taking any type of revenge on his brothers, but by treating them harshly he was able to find out that his father and younger brother were still alive. His harshness also resulted in his brothers coming to grips with what they had done to him so many years earlier; hopefully making them feel guilty enough to ask God for forgiveness.

Before they left Egypt, Joseph ordered their bags to be filled with grain, along with the silver they brought to pay for it. Upon their return home, the brothers discovered the money hidden in the grain and were frightened by this. It caused great consternation for Jacob as well, lamenting the loss first of Joseph and now Simeon. He was adamant that Benjamin would stay home when the time came for them to procure more grain. Talk about family disunity. I imagine there was a lot of finger-pointing between their return home from Egypt and when they had to return for more grain (Genesis 42:25-38).

Lord, these were tumultuous times for Joseph and his family. I don't know all the intricate details of what was going through their minds as these events unfolded, but I do know that Your plan was being implemented. May I be like Joseph and trust that no matter how things seem to be going, good or bad, that You have everything under control. In the name of Jesus, I pray. Amen.

DAY 94

PREPARING THE WAY
Read Genesis 43 - 44:13

Joseph's brothers must have been shaking in their boots at the thought of returning to Egypt. How would they explain the money found in their grain bags from their first visit? Even though their father agreed to let Benjamin go with them, they didn't know what would happen to him, or themselves. They'd already lied to Jacob about Joseph being killed by a wild animal, and they knew he didn't want to lose Benjamin. It wasn't looking good for the brothers, but they knew they had to go or starve (Genesis 43:1-14).

Upon their arrival in Egypt, Joseph saw them coming with Benjamin and told his steward to take them to his house and prepare a meal for them. This was very different from their first encounter with Joseph and filled them with fear. They tried explaining to Joseph's steward what happened with the silver and how they came with double the money and gifts to show it was unintentional. He told them to look at it as a gift from God and not to worry about it (Genesis 43:15-23). How would you have felt about this? I would have been like, "What? What is going on," especially as the steward began leading them into the dining room.

To add to their fear and amazement, Joseph instructed his steward that his brothers be seated at the table in their birth order (Genesis 43:33). By this time I know I'd be looking for a way of escape. It's just too weird, but they had nowhere to go.

When Joseph showed up, they were eager to present their gifts, bowing down before him to the ground. As a teenager, Joseph had two dreams that this would happen one day, and this was the second time they bowed before him. Now it was Joseph's turn to be amazed (Genesis 43:26).

Joseph inquired about his father Jacob, but when he was introduced to Benjamin he couldn't contain himself, leaving the room for his private chamber where he wept. Getting control of himself, he returned and ordered the food to be served, with Benjamin receiving five times the amount of food as his brothers. Eyebrows must have lifted with curiosity as the hum of muffled whispers filled the air with questions of what exactly was happening to them. But they soon relaxed and enjoyed a delightful feast. At dawn the next day, the brothers packed their donkeys and left. Little did they know their good fortune was about to change when Joseph's steward came chasing after them accusing them of stealing Joseph's silver cup. Of course, they had no idea what Joseph had done and so they adamantly denied doing such a thing. But there it was hidden in the grain sack of Benjamin. Fear fell on these men, causing them such great distress that they tore their clothes, an "expression of strong emotion such as shame, anger or mourning" (Genesis 43:27-34).[1]

Have you ever done something in your life that you regret so badly, you wish you could go back and change it? That's not possible, is it? We don't have the privilege of erasing our past and getting a do-over. Life is funny that way. We only get one time around. When we do something that we know is wrong, if we don't make every effort to make it right, it will nag at us, perhaps even impinge on everything we think, do and say.

That's what it was like for Joseph's brothers. All these years they lived with the knowledge that they made it possible for their brother Joseph to be taken away from them. They had no idea where he was taken or if he was even alive. The moment the tables were turned on them, they remembered Joseph and assumed that what was happening to them was because of what they had done to him.

Thank the good Lord, it doesn't have to be that way any longer. If we confess our sins, He is faithful and just and will forgive us our sins and purify us from all unrighteousness (1 John 1:9). We don't have to live with the guilt caused by things we've done wrong, and if an opportunity arises to ask those we have sinned against to forgive us as well, we are doubly blessed.

Lord, may I learn from the mistakes of others as I continue reading through Your Word. Cause me to consider the consequences of my actions when I make decisions. Help me always to choose that which honors and glorifies You. And when I do sin against You and others, help me to be quick to repent and ask for forgiveness. In the precious name of Jesus, I pray. Amen.

DAY 95

JOSEPH'S IDENTITY REVEALED
Read Genesis 44:14-45:24

Judah's desperate plea for Benjamin's freedom is in such contrast to when the brothers allowed Joseph to be sold, it's hard to believe he would fight so tenaciously. Judah pleaded and begged for Benjamin's release, explaining to Joseph that their father would die if Benjamin did not return with them. It's not clear if this is what Joseph was looking for, but it's the result he got. He was so moved by the love shown toward Benjamin, he could no longer contain himself and ordered all of his attendants to leave the room. Then he revealed himself to his brothers and began to weep uncontrollably (Genesis 44:14 - 45:2).

Except for the wails of Joseph, there must have been an atmosphere of almost surreal and utter disbelief at what Joseph was saying. The more Joseph talked, the more convinced they became that yes, indeed, this was actually their little brother that they had taken for dead. Can you even imagine their emotions, from disbelief, to acceptance, to excitement, to all-out rejoicing? Instead of solemn and sad, it became party time with Benjamin receiving the biggest and longest hug from his big brother (Genesis 45:3-14).

The noise from that room must have been deafening for it wasn't long until Pharaoh found out that Joseph's brothers were in Egypt and for the first time in years they were reunited. Pharaoh could hardly contain his excitement and began pouring out blessing after blessing upon Joseph's brothers, instructing them to go back, gather everyone and return to Egypt, where they would be given the best land. Their good fortune continued as they were given carts and provision for the journey home, as well as clothing, donkeys, grain and bread. As they left Egypt, Joseph gave them an admonition, for he must have seen their inclinations already, and he told them, "Don't quarrel on the way" (Genesis 45:16-24).

What would have happened if Joseph's brothers had the same callous attitude toward Benjamin as they did Joseph? The outcome would have been much different. Something happened to them throughout the years. We can imagine that there were guilty whispers among themselves about what they had done to Joseph. That's a heavy burden of guilt to carry around for twenty-plus years. Their attitudes toward each other, their father, and their youngest brother must have softened, realizing that family is important and, in order to remain a family, they had to stick together.

Once Joseph revealed himself to his brothers, he told them, "And now, do not be distressed and do not be angry with yourselves for selling me here, because it was to save lives that God sent me ahead of you...God sent me ahead of you to preserve for you a remnant on earth and to save your lives by a great deliverance" (Genesis 45:5-7). Joseph was fully aware of God's plan and purpose for his life, and the timing couldn't have been more perfect.

This is not the only time Egypt has been a place of refuge for

God's people at His direction. In Matthew 2:13 an angel of the Lord appeared to Joseph, Mary's husband, in a dream and said, "Get up. Take the child and his mother and escape to Egypt. Stay there until I tell you, for Herod is going to search for the child to kill him." Joseph obeyed, and so was fulfilled what the Lord said through the prophet, "Out of Egypt I called my son" (Hosea 11:1).

It's extraordinary the things God does for His children when they obey. God had a plan all along and He knew what it would take to fulfill that plan. We never see the full picture of God's plan for our lives. We couldn't handle it if we did. Like Sarah, we'd be in a hurry to fulfill it in our own way, and we read how that worked out. Let's relish in the knowledge that when we believe in God, the best course to take is to trust Him, especially when difficult times befall us.

Lord, I rejoice in the knowledge of Your plan to preserve Your people from starvation during a time of famine. May I be ever so diligent in trusting You when hard times befall me. In the name of Jesus, I pray. Amen.

DAY 96

THE JOURNEY FROM CANAAN TO EGYPT
Read Genesis 45:25 - 46:34

What must Jacob have been thinking as he saw his sons approaching? They not only had grain and bread but they had carts and donkeys. The chatter and clatter of those returning to Canaan got louder and louder. In excitement, they came running to their father shouting, "Joseph is alive! He is a ruler in Egypt." "Have you lost your minds? What are you telling me?" was Jacob's response of disbelief. "No, no, it's true, father. Your son Joseph is alive and he has sent us to carry you and all we have back to Egypt to live!" (Genesis 45:25-27). Isn't it ironic that when his sons told him a lie, he believed it, and now that they were telling him the truth, he didn't believe it?

Jacob was finally convinced and agreed to go, but not before stopping in Beersheba to offer sacrifices to the Lord. This is the same place that Abraham and Isaac both called out to God and it seems Jacob was not leaving there until he got answers to some questions, like: "What about the land you promised me and my descendants? If we go to Egypt, is there a possibility my descendants will assimilate into Egyptian culture and refuse to return to Canaan?" These were legitimate concerns considering the covenant God made with Abraham, Isaac, and now Jacob. God assured Jacob in a dream that this was part of His plan and that one day his descendants would surely return. For now, He wanted Jacob to be content knowing that Joseph's own hand would close his eyes (Genesis 46:1-4).

Off they went, 70 in all (Genesis 46:27). Not a very big group of people considering God promised that one day they would be more than the sand on the seashore (Genesis 22:17).

What a sight that must have been for the Egyptians to see what seemed a motley crew of shepherds heading into their land, but Pharaoh invited them to come, so there wasn't a word they could say about it. And come they did. Jacob sent Judah to Joseph to get directions to Goshen and when they arrived, Joseph wasted no time in going to see his father. What a reunion it must have been as Joseph threw his arms around his father and wept for a long time. Jacob was so content with their reunion, he was ready to die right then and there (Genesis 46:28-30).

Joseph's relationship with the Lord was unsurpassed. His actions spoke more than a multitude of words ever could, and there's no doubt Joseph saw the hand of God in this entire scenario, culminating in a joyous reunion, not only with his brothers but with his father, whom he loved.

Isn't that what we as Christians hope for, that great reunion that will one day bring everlasting joy? When we have fought the good fight, as Paul wrote to Timothy, when we have finished the race and kept the faith, we have no fear of death. For there is in store for us the crown of righteousness, which the Lord, the righteous Judge, will award us on that day, and not only us, but also to all who have longed for His appearing" (2 Timothy 4:6-8).

Lord, may I keep my eyes fixed on You, knowing that when my days are over I will see Jesus. There will be no more dying there, only rejoicing in Your kingdom where I dwell with Jesus and all those who have gone before. In His precious name I pray. Amen.

DAY 97

BEING PREPARED
Read Genesis 47

After getting his family settled in Goshen, the choicest land of Egypt, Joseph went about Pharaoh's business as the famine in Egypt and Canaan continued. He continued to sell grain to the people until their money ran out. Then they sold their livestock to him in order to stay alive, then their land and lastly themselves, for they had no means to feed themselves other than the grain Joseph stored up. Meanwhile, Jacob and his family were prospering in Goshen (Genesis 47:13-27).

This might be a good time to stop and consider our own times of famine, whether it be food or something else. Can you think of a time when you felt God nudging you to do something and you sloughed it off, only to regret that decision later? It's certain the Egyptian people did when they realized they too could have been storing up grain for their use the same as Joseph did for Pharaoh. Because they didn't, they were unprepared when the time came.

Today, we don't have so much a food famine in our land as we do a spiritual famine. The word of God is excluded under the guise of separation of church and state, not only from our schools, but from anything having to do with government and the public domain. Yet many of our nation's founding documents clearly point to God's help and intervention. Now we find ourselves unprepared to deal with the crime, immorality, political corruption and drug addiction that is happening in the lives of so many today.

It's never too late, though, to make a change. Perhaps the fear that has gripped our nation during the COVID-19 virus is a wake-up call to Christians everywhere; that it's time to be prepared to meet the needs of those who are seeking answers. There are answers and we have them. We only need to read God's word to know what they are.

Lord, help me listen when You tell me to prepare. I have been so busy doing other things to fill my time, I often neglect that which is most important, my time with You and the reading of Your Word. Forgive me, Father, and help me to wake up to the realization that I am here for Your purposes, that this is not my home and that I need to speak a word of encouragement and love to those whose hearts are crying out for help in a time of famine. In the name of Jesus, I pray. Amen.

DAY 98

JACOB AND HIS GRANDSONS
Read Genesis 48

Jacob knew his days were soon coming to an end. When Joseph got the news, he hurried to see his father, bringing his two sons, Manasseh and Ephraim, with him. Jacob, looking back over his life, gave a recitation of the things most dear to him: God, Rachel and seeing not only Joseph again, but seeing his grandchildren (Genesis 48:11).

This might give us pause to think what it will be like when we are close to death. Lord willing, if we go at an old age and have time to be with family and consider what God did for us, it should be a happy occasion for the family to look back on their loved one's life and remember those things that brought joy, comfort and love because of the knowledge God has given us that He will meet us when we cross over from death to life (John 5:24).

Jacob had two wives and two concubines by which he had

twelve sons and a daughter, but it was Rachel who was most dear to his heart. So getting to see Joseph and his grandchildren brought a double blessing, which Jacob then bestowed upon Manasseh and Ephraim, but not in their order of birth. It's quite interesting that Jacob was the younger son of Isaac, but he received the blessing of the eldest. Now Jacob would confer that same blessing on the youngest of Joseph's sons. Joseph thought his father was making a mistake, and even tried taking his hand away from Ephraim's head, but Jacob assured him that he knew what he was doing and that indeed the younger would be greater than the older (Genesis 48:12-20). This later proved true when it came time to inherit the land of Canaan.

Jacob adopted Joseph's sons as his own, bringing them into the line of Abraham and Isaac, making certain that they would not stay behind in Egypt, but that their descendants would one day occupy the land God promised Jacob would be theirs. Joseph made no further objection to Jacob's blessings on his children.

Isn't this the picture we all want to have when we die, our children and grandchildren at our bedside where we can share with them the goodness God has bestowed upon us in our lifetime? Then, when all is said and done, to hand down the blessing of faith, having peace that one day we can have the hope that we will be together again in God's house forevermore.

Lord, those who came before paved the way for my own journey through life. When I read about how at times they faltered and You always lifted them up, it gives me hope that You will do the same for me. I am easily prone to putting You on the back burner of life when things are going my way. Help me remember that I need You always, in the good and bad times. May I remain faithful until my dying days and may those who come after us do the same. In the precious name of Jesus, I pray. Amen.

DAY 99

JACOB'S BLESSINGS AND DEATH
Read Genesis 49

*I*magine the sibling rivalry that took place in Jacob's family over the years. There must have been bickering and fighting amongst the brothers from four different wives that was, at times, insurmountable. Yet God did not forget them. He brought them out of Canaan during a horrible famine and now they were living in the choicest land of Egypt called Goshen.

Jacob had a few years of peace to enjoy his grandchildren and great-grandchildren, but as is the fate of all of us, it came time for him to die. He called his sons to come to him. From the first-born down, he blessed his sons (sometimes sounding more like a curse), to include their descendants after them.

We begin with Reuben, who slept with Bilhah, Rachel's maidservant. He paid dearly for his unstable ways by having his birthright stripped from him and his descendants. Simeon and Levi, who led the slaughter against Shechem after he raped their sister Dinah, were cursed for their anger and retribution, though their descendants were not totally stripped of their inheritance later.

When we do not allow the Lord to be the judge over wrongdoings, we create more problems, not only for ourselves but for others. Had they left the matter in God's hands, He would have dealt with it justly and fairly, and they would have had a clean conscience.

It is best not to seek retribution when we have been wronged, but remember the admonition to not take revenge, but leave room for God's wrath. For it is written, "It is mine to avenge; I will repay," says the Lord (Romans 12:19).

Judah, fourth in line, is blessed beyond measure, chosen as the line from which the Messiah would come. This is an interesting choice as he was the one who had sex with Tamar, his daughter-in-law, thinking she was a prostitute. If we turn to the book of Matthew in the New Testament, we find Perez, whose mother was Tamar, in the Messianic line.

These people had many faults, none of which are hidden from us. And why is that? We can identify with them because we too have faults. Even as Christians, we say and do things that are not Christ-honoring. Isn't it a joy to know that we can repent and ask our Savior to forgive us of our sins and cleanse us of all unrighteousness (1 John 1:19).

Down the line are Zebulun, Issachar, Dan, Gad, Asher, and Naphtali. Their significance is not diminished because they are not as prominent in the events of history. We don't know as much about these sons as we do the others, but they and their descendants are among the twelve tribes of Israel who are mentioned throughout the Old and New Testaments.

Then there is Joseph, the one man who stands out above all others in the Old Testament. His life parallels that of our Savior in many ways. He was persecuted and hated by his own brothers who sold him into slavery. Jesus was mocked and continually ridiculed by those who did not believe He was the Messiah, and He was sold into their hands for thirty pieces of silver by one of

His own disciples. There is not one hint of unrighteousness, unfaithfulness or distrust about Joseph. No matter his predicament, he never said one harsh word about another person; nor did he blame anything or anyone for his undeserved slavery and imprisonment. He is silent. Jesus, too, was silent as he stood before his accusers.

The most significant parallel is that Joseph was taken from the pits of hell basically, the jail in which he was imprisoned, and given the most prominent position in Egypt, second in command to the Pharaoh. Jesus was murdered on a cross. He spent three days in the tomb and, on the third day, He rose again. Victorious over death, he ascended into heaven where He is now seated at the right hand of God the Father (Colossians 3:1).

Christianity is not some rigid form of religion. It is a real and personal relationship with the person of Jesus Christ, the Son of God. We should be thankful to those who came before us, the ones who paved the way for the most cataclysmic event in this world to take place; the birth, life, death, and resurrection of our Savior!

Holy Spirit, may I call upon You to help me with my weaknesses and hardships. Help me always to be mindful of Your presence and not forget the hope to which I am called. Help me remember that my struggle is not against flesh and blood but against the rulers, against the authorities, against the powers of this dark world and against the spiritual forces of evil in the heavenly realms. Help me fight the good fight so that on the day Jesus returns, I am found faithful. Amen.

DAY 100

DEATHS OF JACOB AND JOSEPH
Read Genesis 50

Jacob's death brought such great sorrow upon Joseph that he threw himself onto Jacob's dead body, and he wept (Genesis 50:1). I know what it's like to lose your dad, and it is a sorrowful time. The person who brought you into this world is now gone, and life will never be the same.

Like Joseph, I too was separated, not only from my dad but my entire family, even for much longer than Joseph. When we reunited, it was a sweet time together for us, and I'm so grateful to God for making that possible.

Jacob's one request of Joseph was that after he died, he wanted to be buried in the land of Canaan where his father and grandfather were buried. When Joseph explained the situation to Pharaoh, he not only honored Joseph's request, he sent some of his own people to accompany Joseph and his family (Genesis 50:2-8). Pharaoh was so grateful to Joseph, he denied him nothing when he asked.

Jacob was carried back to the land of Canaan and buried in the cave in the field of Machpelah, near Mamre, which Abraham bought as a burial place. He was buried next to Abraham, Isaac and his wife Leah. After his burial, Joseph, his brothers and all who went with them returned to Egypt. Burying a loved one is always difficult, but life goes on for those left behind.

His brothers still carried a great amount of guilt and were fearful that now that their father was dead, Joseph would take retribution on them. They sent word to Joseph, "Your father left instructions before he died: This is what you are to say to Joseph: I ask you to forgive your brothers the sins and wrongs they committed in treating you so badly..." When Joseph received this message, he wept. We don't know why he wept. Perhaps he was hurt that his brothers still thought he would take revenge on them for what they did so many years earlier (Genesis 50:15-17).

It's not much different today. When we've done something wrong and it goes unresolved, the guilt that comes with the wrongdoing can eat away at us until it consumes us. Let's not be like Joseph's brothers and live with that guilt. Let's get on our knees before Jesus and ask Him to set us free from the sin that entangles us. And, if possible, seek forgiveness from the one we have wronged. Then we can live guilt-free.

Joseph, in his tender and mild way of saying things, assured his brothers not to be afraid but to remember that, "You intended to harm me, but God intended it for good to accomplish what is now being done, the saving of many lives. Do not be afraid. I will provide for you and your children" (Genesis 50:19-20).

Some of us go through much more difficult and trying times than others, and it may even seem unbearable to endure, but as Christians, we are told to trust the Lord and not lean on our own understanding of things, but in all our ways acknowledge Him, and He will make our paths straight (Proverbs 3:5-6). Joseph did, and look what happened to him!

Joseph died at the age of one hundred and ten years old. He made the sons of Israel swear an oath and said, "God will surely come to your aid, and then you must carry my bones up from this place." Little did he know it would be 400 years until this would take place: Joseph's bones, which the Israelites brought up from Egypt, were buried at Shechem in the tract of land that Jacob bought for 100 pieces of silver from the sons of Hamor, the father of Shechem. This became the inheritance of Joseph's descendants (Joshua 24:32).

Lord, whatever my sorrow, whatever my pain, keep me always mindful of what someone else intended for evil, You, O Lord, intended for good. As I reflect upon the lives of Jacob and Joseph, may I be reminded of the unsurpassed love You have for Your people. May my heart be filled to overflowing with the knowledge that You are Almighty God, the Creator of all things, and that my destiny is in Your hands. In the holy name of Jesus, I pray. Amen.

AFTERWORD

Our Identity In Genesis

It's been a long journey through the book of Genesis. I pray you've been strengthened in faith and blessed in spirit. As we conclude, I ask you to ponder these questions:

- Have you come to an understanding that you are important to the Lord God Almighty, the Creator of Heaven and earth?
- Do you have an understanding that you are here on earth, in this place, at this very time, because this is where God intended you to be?
- Have you felt connected to those who blazed the path before us, making the way for the Messiah to come so that we could be reunited with our heavenly Father after Adam and Eve rebelled against Him and brought sin into the world?
- Do you realize the intricate plan of salvation that God Almighty implemented just for you?

If some of these questions are hard to answer, then perhaps there are unresolved wounds in your life that need to be dealt with in an open and honest way.

There is no better way to do that than to be on your knees before the King of kings and Lord of lords, humbling yourself before Him and asking Him to not only forgive you, but to heal your brokenness and set you free so that you can be the person He made you to be, and you can live the life He intends for You to live.

He has given us the tools to do it. It began in Genesis and continues all the way through to Revelation where we know how the story ends. For those who believe in the Lord Jesus Christ as the Son of God, the Savior of the world, the Redeemer of Israel—the One who died on a cross, was buried, rose again and is seated at the right hand of God—the war has been won and victory is ours for all of eternity! Is that not a glorious promise? Is that not something to shout about and praise the Lord for?

The book of Revelation ends with some of the most reassuring words of our Lord Jesus Christ. He said,

> Behold, I am coming soon! My reward is with Me and I will give to everyone according to what he has done. I am the Alpha and the Omega, the First and the Last, the Beginning and the End. Blessed are those who wash their robes, that they may have the right to the tree of life and may go through the gates into the city (New Jerusalem). Outside are the dogs, those who practice magic arts, the sexually immoral, the murderers, the idolaters and everyone who loves and practices falsehood. I, Jesus, have sent my angel to give you this testimony for the churches. I am the Root and the Offspring of David, the bright and Morning Star... Yes, I am coming soon.
>
> —Revelation 22:12-16, 20

Now the dwelling of God is with men, and He will live with them. They will be His people, and God himself will be with them and be their God. He will wipe every tear from their eyes. There will be no more death or mourning or crying or pain, for the old order of things has passed away (Revelation 21:3-4).

Everything that happened in Genesis set the trails blazing toward this very end. Those whom we came to know and love in the first book of the Bible will be in heaven waiting to greet us. Then we will be together forevermore.

NOTES

5. DAY 5

1. Nevins, Stuart 1974. Planet Earth: Plan or Accident? Acts & Facts. 3 (5). http://www.icr.org/article/planet-earth-plan-or-accident/

28. DAY 28

1. https://www.quora.com/What-does-Eber-mean-in-Hebrew
   The name Eber is first found in Genesis 10:21 - *Unto Shem also, the father of all the children of **Eber**...* (KJV)
   In Hebrew this name is written as עבר (*ever*, Strong's #5677) and is derived from the verb עבר (*Ah.B.R*, Strong's 5674), which means "to cross over" or "to pass through." The noun derived from this verb is עבר (*ever*, Strong's #5676) and means "the other side" and this is also the meaning of the name Eber.
   A person that is descended from Eber is called an עברי (*eevriy* - Hebrew), which literally means "one of Eber." A group of people descended from Eber are called עברים (*eevriym* – Hebrews).

29. DAY 29

1. https://www.ethnologue.com/guides/how-many-languages

52. DAY 52

1. Pawson, David. Sermon Old Testament Studies: Genesis 21 https://www.davidpawson.org/resources/resource/761?return_url=https%3A%2F%2Fwww.davidpawson.org%2Fresources%2Fcategory%2Fold-testament-studies%2Fgenesis%2F

53. DAY 53

1. M. G. Easton, M.A., D.D., Illustrated Bible Dictionary, Third Edition, Published by Thomas Nelson, 1897 www.biblestudytools.com/dictionary/beersheba

56. DAY 56

1. The NIV Matthew Henry Commentary in One Volume, 1992, page 43

57. DAY 57

1. Marshall, Taylor, 2008, Testimony and Testicles - The Oath of Abraham's Servant - https://taylormarshall.com/2008/testimony-testicles-oath-of.html

61. DAY 61

1. Pawson, David. Sermon Old Testament Studies: Genesis 24 https://www.davidpawson.org/resources/resource/758?return_url=https%3A%2F%2Fwww.davidpawson.org%2Fresources%2Fcategory%2Fold-testament-studies%2Fgenesis%2F

62. DAY 62

1. Wikipedia. 2020. "Ishmael." Last modified June 15, 2020. https://en.wikipedia.org/wiki/Ishmael

68. DAY 68

1. Deffinbaugh, Robert. May 12, 2004. "From Paradise to Patriarchs, Working Like the Devil Serving the Lord."
   https://bible.org/seriespage/28-working-devil-serving-lord-genesis-271-46

71. DAY 71

1. Hobson, Tom. October 12, 2017. "What was Wrong with Leah's Eyes?" https://www.patheos.com/blogs/tomhobson/2017/10/wrong-leahs-eyes/

78. DAY 78

1. Henry, Matthew. *The NIV Matthew Henry Commentary in One Volume*, 1992. page 55, verses 9-12.
   "Times of fear should be times of prayer; whatever frightens us should drive us to our knees, to our God."

81. DAY 81

1. Easton, M. G. *Illustrated Bible Dictionary*, *Third Edition*. Nashville: Thomas Nelson, 1897. https://www.biblestudytools.com/dictionary/el-elohe-Isreal

84. DAY 84

1. Got Questions Ministries. "What Do We Know About the Edomites?" 2020. https://www.compellingtruth.org/Edomites.html

88. DAY 88

1. The Holy Bible, New International Version 2005, Zondervan, 35.

89. DAY 89

1. Henry, Matthew. Matthew Henry's Commentary on the Whole Bible (Complete). Vol. 1. M.p. 1706. Page 62. http://www.biblestudytools.com/commentaries/matthew-henry-complete/genesis/
2. Congreve, William. *The Mourning Bride*.
3. *NIV Cultural Backgrounds Study Bible.* (Zondervan, 2016). https://theholymess.com/3-bible-verses-for-when-you-are-falsely-accused/
   for suggestions on Scripture when falsely accused of something

90. DAY 90

1. Cook, Matthew, Feb 24, 2005, "The Cupbearer & The Baker," Sermon. https://www.sermoncentral.com/sermons/the-cupbearer-the-baker-matthew-cook-sermon-on-god-s-omniscience-76727?page=2&wc=800

92. DAY 92

1. Bible Truth, "Zaphnath-Paaneah." https://bibletruthpublishers.com/zaphnath-paaneah/ljm16847
2. *NIV Cultural Backgrounds Study Bible.* (Zondervan, 2016), 91.

94. DAY 94

1. Oladokun, Sarah. June 8, 2017. "Why did People in the Old Testament Tear Their Robes?" https://www.christiantoday.com/article/why-did-people-in-the-old-testament-tear-their-robes/109889.htm

ABOUT THE AUTHOR

Mindi Colchico Wroblewski is a retired court reporter who worked 15 years in the federal court system and 10 years as an Official Reporter of Debates on Capitol Hill for both the House and the Senate. She married late in life to Tom, and they presently live in Port St. Lucie, Florida. They are blessed with two children, three grandchildren, and one great-granddaughter.

Throughout her life, Mindi has been a lover of words. As a child, she enjoyed writing many letters to friends and family, and as a court reporter, she has written articles for both the United States Court Reporters Association and the National Court Reporters Association. In her career, she's written hundreds of thousands of words of the both the famous and the infamous while working in the United States Federal Court in Washington, DC., the US Federal Court in San Diego, California, and in Congress as an Official Reporter of Debates--but her love for words hasn't stopped there. She has also written many unpublished short stories about her travels to parts of Europe and around the United States, honing her skills of description to bring her readers to places they might never visit.

This love for language, combined with her love for God, culminated in Mindi's present endeavors as an author of Christian non-fiction. In 2013, she self-published a devotional on Psalms, Proverbs, and the New Testament called *A Daily Devotional of God's Unending Love*. *Daily Reflections*, the book you are now holding, is a first in a series of devotionals she plans to write on the Old Testament.